The Development of

GERMANIC VERSE FORM

WINFRED P. LEHMANN

The Development of Germanic Verse Form

GORDIAN PRESS
NEW YORK
1971

Originally Published 1956
Reprinted 1971

Copyright © 1956 by
UNIVERSITY OF TEXAS PRESS
PUBLISHED BY GORDIAN PRESS, INC.
By Arrangement

Library of Congress Catalog Card Number - 70-131252
ISBN 87752-014-3

PREFACE

An understanding of Germanic verse form is rare among students of literature even after they have been exposed to courses in Old English, Old Norse, or the other older Germanic languages. Even though it is easy to demonstrate a greater refinement of form in *Beowulf* than in most subsequent English poetry, one frequently encounters views no more informed than those of Edith Sitwell (quoted in Chapter 6) that Germanic poetry was "crude and unskilled" in form. Such views may be the result of the approach used in the teaching of old literary works, for these works are generally treated as repositories of linguistic and philological lore; students in a *Beowulf* course, for example, may master more types of metrical arrangements than lines of the poem. When attention is devoted to the linguistic form of the notable Germanic works, it commonly centers about identification of the declension to which a noun may belong, the ablaut class according to which a verb is inflected, or the subdialect in which the work has survived, with no regard to the patterns that display stylistic or poetic excellence. Surrounded by such teaching, neither Miss Sitwell's pronouncements nor the general opinion about Germanic poetry can surprise us.

In the present study, poetic form is dealt with as one facet of Germanic culture which varied as that culture was modified. Such an approach should contribute more to an

v

aesthetic understanding of Germanic poetry than do many of the previous formal studies which make the analysis of poetic form their primary end. For unless we view poetic form as a structure influenced by other cultural elements, primarily linguistic, we cannot determine whether a poet was conservative or innovating, capable or mediocre, a master or a servant of his form. It is true that the form of poetry at certain periods more than at others and in the hands of certain authors is more satisfying aesthetically to us. But even as students of literature we must attempt to understand forms that do not appeal to us and to note the processes of development from cruder to more elegant forms, and the reverse. The better understanding of Germanic verse form resulting from such a study must lead to a more accurate appraisal of Germanic poetry.

Much of the material for this book was collected and much of the writing done in 1950–51 while I was in Norway on a Fulbright fellowship. I wish to express to the Department of State and to the Fulbright administrators my deepest appreciation for the leisure that made possible my study and my acquaintance with a culture and with men to whom Germanic poetry and culture is not as remote as it is in this country. Especially to Professor Carl J. S. Marstrander and to Hallvard Bergwitz am I grateful: to Professor Marstrander for his formal and informal discussions of Germanic culture, notably of the runic inscriptions; to Mr. Bergwitz for an introduction to the elements of Germanic culture that are still alive in Norway.

Ruth P. Lehmann, Lee M. Hollander, Helmut Rehder, and A. A. Hill have read the manuscript in various stages. I thank them for many suggestions and corrections. Harcourt, Brace and Company, Inc., has kindly granted permission to include the quotation from the verse of T. S. Eliot. I also wish to express my gratitude to the firm of Pearn, Pollinger

& Higham, Ltd., for permitting me to quote the excerpt from the work of Dame Edith Sitwell. A grant from the Research Council of the University of Texas has made publication possible.

WINFRED P. LEHMANN

Austin, Texas

NOTES ON SOURCES

Textual study and the editions of the past decades have not consistently aided the appreciation of Germanic verse. The lack of suitable texts presents one of the greatest difficulties in the study of old Germanic literature. Fifty years ago the student of literature was more fortunate than are we today; at that time collections were available which combined all the poetry of one period in a few volumes. Anyone who wished to read the Old English alliterative works, for example, found them all assembled in the *Bibliothek der Angelsächsischen Poesie* of C. W. M. Grein and R. P. Wülcker and B. Assman (Kassel-Leipzig, 1881–98). Similar collections existed for Old Norse verse and for Middle High German lyric poetry. Since then we have been provided with authoritative texts which are based on scholarly analyses so voluminous that for some works at least one page of commentary exists for every word of the text. One of the standard editions of the *Beowulf*, Fr. Klaeber's 3d ed. (Boston, 1936), presents the text of the poem in 120 pages and supporting material in three times as many; subsequent printings have incorporated even more notes. Other Old English texts have received similarly ample treatment. Accordingly, anyone who wishes to read Old English today feels constrained by his scholarly conscience to equip himself with a shelf full of texts

rather than with the few convenient volumes that his predecessors might have used. A similar situation exists for all
the Germanic literary works, not only for the Old English.

Moreover, the modern critical texts have been designed
for any purpose but the reader's enjoyment. The standard
text of the poems of Walther von der Vogelweide is that
edited by Karl Lachman, 10th ed. by Carl von Kraus (Berlin
and Leipzig, 1936). A more repelling text would be difficult
to imagine. Von Kraus's scalpel is evident in every line. It is
hardly surprising therefore that today university students,
not only in America but also abroad, accept their quota of old
Germanic literature as a dose of unpleasant medicine, and that
critics make absurd remarks about old Germanic literature
which may influence some readers but which chiefly indicate
the innocence of the critics. If any but linguistic surgeons are
to continue reading old Germanic poetry, we will have to
produce editions in reasonably attractive form with the helps
to understanding that some of the voluminous critical work
of the past century have produced, but without the scholarly
trappings that may indicate the extent of the editor's learning
but only hinder an understanding of the text. One useful
volume has been published recently, *A Middle High German
Courtly Reader* by M. Joos and F. R. Whitesell (Madison,
1951), but this contains only selected texts, not a complete
work nor all the lyric poetry of one author or of one period.
When similar texts have been provided for the superior Germanic literary works, the Old Norse *Edda,* the *Beowulf,*
Gottfried's *Tristan,* Wolfram's *Parzival,* we may expect that
a few readers will find enjoyment in this early literature, and
that an occasional critic will read it before voicing his pronouncements.

For this study of Germanic verse form one of the various
standard editions has been chosen, and quotations are based
on it. The other standard editions are listed in this preface

along with a selection of the critical literature in which data on further editions and further critical material may be found.

No attempt has been made to collect the oldest Germanic verse in one volume. The first beginnings of poetry, found in the runic inscriptions, may best be consulted in Wolfgang Krause's *Runeninschriften im älteren Futhark* (Halle, 1937). Various scholars have, however, dealt critically with the oldest Germanic literature. In spite of their age, the two best works in English are those of W. P. Ker: in *The Dark Ages* (Edinburgh and London, 1904) he deals with all the literary products of the early period, including the Latin; in *Epic and Romance* (2d ed., London, 1908) he traces the development from the early Germanic verse and its ideals until these were modified through the influence of Christian and Romance thought. More complete and thorough than Ker's books, and restricted to the earliest Germanic verse, is Andreas Huesler's *Die altgermanische Dichtung* (2d ed., Potsdam, 1941), which is unsurpassed for this period.

All of the Old English alliterative verse may be found in Grein-Wülcker and in *The Anglo-Saxon Poetic Records,* ed. in 6 vols. by G. P. Krapp and Elliott van Kirk Dobbie (New York, 1932–53); the *Beowulf* and the *Fight at Finnsburg* (or *Finn's Borough*) have been cited from Klaeber's text.

Numerous translations of Old English verse are available, especially of the *Beowulf;* twenty-four versions are listed with evaluation by Klaeber (cxxx–cxxxii), and some have appeared since. A convenient collection of translated Old English verse is that of R. K. Gordon, *Anglo-Saxon Poetry Selected and Translated,* vol. 794 of "Everyman's Library"; the translations are in prose.

Of the various treatments of Old English literature possibly the most useful recent one is that by Kemp Malone in *A Literary History of England,* ed. by A. C. Baugh (New York and London, 1948).

Middle English verse is not conveniently available in any small series of texts. Citations here have been made from *Middle English Metrical Romances,* ed. by Walter H. French and Charles B. Hale (New York, Prentice-Hall, Inc., 1930), except that lines of Layamon have been cited from Sir Frederick Madden's *Laȝamon's Brut or Chronicles of Britain* (3 vols., London, 1847) and those of *Gawain* from *Sir Gawain and the Green Knight,* ed. by J. R. R. Tolkien and E. V. Gordon (Oxford, 1936 reprint). The notable Middle English lyric verse may be found variously in collections, some even in *The Oxford Book of English Verse,* chosen and edited by Arthur Quiller-Couch.

A concise recent treatment of Middle English verse may be found in *A Literary History of England,* written by the editor A. C. Baugh. Of great importance for the study of Middle English alliterative verse are two books by J. P. Oakden, *Alliterative Poetry in Middle English: The Dialectal and Metrical Survey* (Manchester, 1930) and *Alliterative Poetry in Middle English: A Survey of the Traditions,* with assistance from E. R. Innes (Manchester, 1935). Noteworthy also are Karl Schumacher's *Studien über den Stabreim in der mittelenglischen Alliterationsdichtung,* Bonner Studien zur englischen Philologie, XI (Bonn, 1914), and the essay of M. Stobie, "The Influence of Morphology on Middle English Alliterative Poetry," *The Journal of English and Germanic Philology,* 39 (1940), 319–36.

A representative selection of Old High German verse may be found in Wilhelm Braune's *Althochdeutsches Lesebuch,* 11th ed., prepared by Karl Helm (Halle, 1949), which is particularly valuable for its bibliographies. Selections from Otfrid have been taken from *Otfrids Evangelienbuch,* ed. by Oskar Erdmann (Halle, 1882). Selections from the late Old High German period have been taken from Karl Müllenhoff and Wilhelm Scherer's *Denkmäler Deutscher Poesie und*

Prosa aus dem VIII-XII. Jahrhundert, by Elias v. Steinmeyer (3d ed., Berlin, 1892). The standard literary history
of this period is the first volume of Gustav Ehrismann's
*Geschichte der deutschen Literatur bis zum Ausgang des
Mittelalters* (2d ed., München, 1932).

Middle High German epic verse has been cited from
various editions: Wolfram von Eschenbach's *Parzival* from
the edition of A. Leitzmann, 2d and 3d eds. (Halle, 1903–28);
Gottfried von Strassburg's *Tristan und Isolt* from the only
English edition, an incomplete one, however, by August
Closs (Oxford, 1947); the *Nibelungenlied* from the 12th ed.
of Karl Bartsch's text, prepared by Helmut de Boor (Leipzig, 1949). The early medieval lyrics are cited from *Des
Minnesangs Frühling* (referred to as *MF*), the latest edition
of which was prepared by Carl von Kraus (Leipzig, 1944).
Walther's poems from Karl Lachmann's *Gedichte Walthers
von der Vogelweide,* the 10th ed. of which was prepared by
Carl von Kraus (Berlin and Leipzig, 1936). Late courtly
lyrics are cited from F. von der Hagen's *Minnesinger* (4
vols., Leipzig, 1838); this now is superseded by Carl von
Kraus's *Deutsche Liederdichter des 13. Jahrhunderts* (Tü-
bingen, 1951——) and the individual editions cited by Von
Kraus.

Numerous translations of medieval poetry have been
made; recent ones are *The "Tristan and Isolde" of Gottfried
von Strassburg* by Edwin H. Zeydel (Princeton, 1948) and
The Parzival of Wolfram von Eschenbach by Edwin H.
Zeydel in collaboration with B. Q. Morgan (Chapel Hill,
1951).

For background material on medieval German poetry
one may best consult the second to fourth volumes of Ehrismann's *Geschichte* (München, 1922–35). Access to the tremendous number of textual studies of the early lyric poetry
and of Walther may most easily be gained through Carl von

Kraus's 'investigations': *Des Minnesangs Frühling, Untersuchungen* (Leipzig, 1939), referred to below as *MFU,* and *Walther von der Vogelweide, Untersuchungen* (Berlin 1935).

The Old Saxon poetry has been cited from Otto Behaghel's *Heliand und Genesis,* the 6th ed. of which was prepared by Walther Mitzka (Halle, 1948). The introduction of this presents a thorough bibliography with discussion of important critical work. An English translation has been prepared by the Reverend Robert G. Philip.

Numerous editions of the Old Norse poetry have been published, each with varying merit and adherents. The *Edda* is here cited from the third edition of G. Neckel (Heidelberg, 1936), Skaldic verse from Finnur Jónsson's edition, *Den Norsk-Islandske Skjaldedigtning* (Copenhagen, 1904–15). The selection from late Icelandic verse has been taken from Th. Wisén's *Riddara-Rímur* (Copenhagen, 1881). Selections from the sagas have been taken from Guðni Jónsson's Islendinga sögur: *Egils saga Skalla-grímssonar* and *Njáls saga* (Reykjavík, 1945).

Translations of selections from Old Norse verse and prose may be found in Henry Goddard Leach's *A Pageant of Old Scandinavia* (Princeton, 1946), which presents translations by a great number of authors, giving also a list of available translations. All the poems of the *Edda* have been translated by Lee M. Hollander, *The Poetic Edda* (Austin, 1928). Access to the difficult Skaldic poetry may be found most easily in Lee M. Hollander's *The Skalds* (Princeton, 1947), a fine book that should be followed by presentations of other Germanic genres, such as the heroic ode.

The most comprehensive literary history of the northern material is Finnur Jónsson's *Den oldnorske og oldislandske Litteraturs Historie* (3 vols., 2d ed., Copenhagen, 1920–24). A less constrained view of the origins of Skaldic verse may be found in Sophus Bugge's *Bidrag til den aeldste Skjalde-digtnings Historie* (Christiania, 1894).

Besides the general works listed above, various important works have been published on single subjects. Versification was first dealt with in detail by Eduard Sievers in *Altgermanische Metrik* (Halle, 1893), a book which has not been superseded even by the second edition which was prepared by Fr. Kauffmann and Hugo Gering (Strassburg, 1905). A second highly important work for the study of Germanic versification is A. Heusler's *Deutsche Versgeschichte mit Einschluss des altenglischen und altnordischen Stabreimverses* (3 vols., Berlin and Leipzig, 1925–29). Views similar to Heusler's were developed independently in this country by William Ellery Leonard; these may be found conveniently in "Four Footnotes to Papers on Germanic Metrics," *Studies in English Philology, A Miscellany in Honor of Frederick Klaeber,* ed. by Kemp Malone *et al.* (Minneapolis, 1929), 1–13. A tremendous number of works on Germanic versification have been published, especially in the nineteenth century; those interested will find ample references in Sievers and Heusler. For a general work on English versification one may consult George Saintsbury, *A History of English Prosody from the Twelfth Century to the Present Day* (3 vols., London, 1906–10). In Wilhelm Meyer's *Gesammelte Abhandlungen zur Mittellateinischen Rythmik* (3 vols., Berlin, 1905–36) one may find essays dealing with the form of the little-known early medieval Latin poetry which is of great importance for its effect on various national verse forms. For Irish metrics unfortunately nothing more ample or reliable has been published than Kuno Meyer's *A Primer of Irish Metrics* (Dublin, 1909). A comparative essay is H. Spanke's "Romanische und mittellateinische Formen in der Metrik von Minnesangs Frühling," *Zeitschrift für romanische Philologie,* 49 (1929), 191–235.

Numerous monographs also deal with the development of rime, among them Ulrich Pretzel's *Frühgeschichte des deutschen Reims*, Palaestra 220 (Leipzig, 1941) and Carl Wesle's *Frühmittelhochdeutsche Reimstudien*, Jenaer Germanistische Forschungen, 9 (Jena, 1925). An example of a prosodic investigation of one poem may be found in T. Gregory Foster's *Judith. Studies in Metre, Language and Style*, Quellen und Forschungen, 71 (Strassburg, 1892).

The best essay on the origin of alliteration is Carl J. S. Marstrander's "Notes on Alliteration," which unfortunately is published in a relatively inaccessible book, *Serta Eitremiana* (Oslo, 1942), 185–207. Among other studies of alliteration we may mention H. Wenck's "Zur alliteration im Eddischen Fornyrðislag," *PBB*, 31 (1906), 91–238, Ragnar Hollmérus' *Studier över alliterationen i Eddan*, Skrifter utgivna av Svenska Litteratursällskapet i Finnland, CCLVIII (Helsingfors, 1936), and W. P. Lehmann's *The Alliteration of Old Saxon Poetry*, Suppl. 3 to *Norsk Tidsskrift For Sprogvidenskap* (Oslo, 1953). J. Lawrence's *Chapters on Alliterative Verse* (London, 1893) deals perceptively with various prosodic subjects in Old English verse.

General stylistic matters have been dealt with by R. Heinzel in his short book *Über den Stil der altgermanischen Poesie*, Quellen und Forschungen 10 (Strassburg, 1875) and in greater detail by Richard M. Meyer in *Die altgermanische Poesie nach ihren formelhaften Elementen beschrieben* (Berlin, 1889), The characteristic stylistic feature of Old Norse verse, the *kenning*, has also been treated variously; compare R. Meissner's *Die Kenningar der Skalden* (Bonn und Leipzig, 1921) and W. Mohr's *Kenningstudien* (Stuttgart, 1933).

Excellent stylistic studies are Günther Müller's "Studien zum Formproblem des Minnesangs," *Deutsche Vierteljahrsschrift für Literaturwissenschaft und Geistesgeschichte*, 1

(1923), 61–103; Ludwig Wolff's "Über den Stil der altgermanischen Poesie," *ibid.*, 214–29, and Eduard Schröder's
"Steigerung und häufung der alliteration in der westgermanischen dichtung. I. Die anwendung alliterierender nominal composita," in *Zeitschrift für deutsches Altertum und
deutsche Litteratur*, 43 (1899), 361–85.

Examples of the oldest Irish poetry may be found in
three monographs by Kuno Meyer: *Über die älteste irische
Dichtung I* and *II*, Abhandlungen der Königlichen preussischen Akademie der Wissenschaften, Phil.-Hist. Kl. (Berlin,
1913), and *Bruchstücke der älteren Lyrik Irlands*, Abhandlungen der preussischen Akademie der Wissenschaften (Berlin, 1919). W. Krause has dealt with a comparison of the use
of the *kenning* in Celtic and Germanic poetry in *Die Kenning
als typische Stilfigur der germanischen und keltischen Dich-
tersprache*. Schriften der Königsberger Gelehrten Gesellschaft.
Geisteswissenschaftliche Kl. 7.1 (Halle, 1930).

Discussions of medieval music may be found in H. E.
Wooldridge, *The Polyphonic Period*, Part I, *Method of Musical Art, 330–1330, The Oxford History of Music* (Oxford,
1901), which now is replaced by *Early Medieval Music up to
1300, New Oxford History of Music*, Vol. II ed. by Dom
Anselm Hughes (London, 1954), and Gustav Reese, *Music
in the Middle Ages* (New York, 1940).

In linguistic matters I have made use of the standard
handbooks, notably: W. Braune and K. Helm, *Althoch-
deutsche Grammatik*, ed. by W. Mitzka (8th ed., Halle,
1953); A. Noreen, *Altisländische Grammatik* (4th ed., Halle,
1923); E. Sievers, *Altenglische Grammatik*, reworked by K.
Brunner (Halle, 1950); F. Holthausen, *Altsächsisches Ele-
mentarbuch* (Heidelberg, 1921).

Numerous other essays and books have been of help in
gaining an understanding and appreciation of the older literature, especially those by Georg Baesecke, C. M. Bowra, Fried-

erich Gennrich, Andreas Heusler, Eduard Sievers, and Ludwig Wolff. One can hardly open a volume of the important periodicals, such as the *Beiträge zur Geschichte der deutschen Sprache und Literatur* (abbreviated *PBB*) and the *Zeitschrift für deutsches Altertum und deutsche Litteratur* (*ZfdA*) with its companion *Anzeiger für deutsches Altertum und deutsche Litteratur* (*AfdA*) without finding an illuminating study of some literary movement, author, or work. It would require many years to exhaust these, and in reading them one is struck by the extent of knowledge of the nineteenth-century scholars and their many acute critical observations, some of which antedate interpretations which a reader has earlier credited to himself.

The translations to poems cited in the text are designed for philological purposes. An attempt, not always successful, was made to indicate in them the form of the original, possibly to the detriment of its sense. Other translations may be found in the works referred to above.

CONTENTS

ERRATA

xi. mid	Huesler	should be	Heusler.
30.7	gāyātri	should be	gāyatrī.
82. mid.	haðuk–	should be	havuk–.

86.10   ǣ ǣ, ā ā, ī ī (oe), u u, ǣ ǣ   should be
         æ   æ æ

      i.e. three macrons should be removed.

98.6 from bottom   fpēodrihten   should be   fēodrihten.

The Development of

GERMANIC VERSE FORM

1 INTRODUCTION

Germanic verse form underwent a tremendous change in the centuries after A.D. 800; the difference in form between poetry written before and after this change is greater than that between any subsequent periods. While the old form gradually became obsolete in all the Germanic languages, the new form has been maintained to the present, as Ker was fond of pointing out by illustrating the modernity of twelfth-century Provençal verse form.

During the period of change the fundamental rhythmic bond of poetry had been transmuted. In the early Germanic poetry it was contained within the line; verses were welded together by means of alliteration (likeness of sound in initial elements of important words of a verse). This likeness was coupled with and strengthened by stress; those segments that were alike were also recited with greatest emphasis. Accordingly, all the elements that unify a line were packed into the same segments. The result was a solemn, slow-moving line of great force.

In later Germanic poetry, when end rime replaced alliteration, the like elements fell at the end of the line; unlike alliteration, end rime did not direct attention to the semantically important elements of the verse, for end rime often was made with words which were relatively unimportant in meaning; the semantically important words were now stressed by

3

other means, such as their position in the sentence and shifts in the rhythm. And rhythm of the verse was divorced from likeness of sound; the accented syllables of a verse could be chosen freely, with no regard to their sound. Now the rhythmic bonds of poetry were diverse; stress patterns had been separated from patterns of rime. On the other hand, the accentual rhythm was much more closely regulated; no longer could the number of unstressed syllables be varied at will. Yet the new form was less demanding than the old.

With this greater freedom of structure Germanic verse had gained in variety of expression but lost in forcefulness. One may note the difference in passages of similar content, as in the following descriptions, the first from the Old English *Beowulf* 991 and the second from the Middle High German *Parzival* 229.23:

Đā wæs hāten hreþe   Heort innanweard
folmum gefrætwod;   fela þǣra wæs,
wera ond wīfa,   þe pæt wīnreced,
gestsele gyredon.   Goldfāg scinon
web æfter wāgum,   wundorsīona fela
secga gehwylcum   þāra þe on swylc stara∂.

    Then speedily came the behest   Heorot within
    with hands to adorn;   a host of them was there,
    of men and women,   who that wine-room,
    that guest-hall decked.   Golden shone
    rugs on the walls,   wondrous sights many
    for each of men   who at them looks.

si giengen ûf einen palas.
hundert krône dâ gehangen was,
vil kerzen drûf gestôzen,
ob den hûsgenôzen,
kleine kerzen alumme an der want.
hundert bette er ligen vant
daz schuofen, dies dâ pflâgen:
hundert kulter drûfe lâgen,
    Into a palace then they went,

where full a hundred crowns suspent,
from which the light of tapers played,
had been arranged by steward and maid,
with candles on the walls around.
A hundred couches there he found
prepared by those who there held sway
and hundred quilts upon them lay, . . .

The rhythm of the *Beowulf* is as rugged and sturdy as the hall it describes; that of the *Parzival,* while hardly dainty, is smoother and more graceful.

Although these changes have not escaped notice, work on them has been cursory; we have no over-all study of the changes themselves, nor of the various forces which may have influenced them. The change from alliteration to end-rime verse is usually depicted as a complete break in tradition, especially in critical works on continental Germanic literature. Yet even on the continent the last alliterative works contain rimes, and in England we find the two forms becoming more and more mixed. And when reasons for changes are proposed, these are usually cultural influences from the outside; W. Scherer[1] ascribed the adoption of end rime to the changes in Germanic life which accompanied the introduction of Christianity. Yet our oldest alliterative work from the continent, the Old Saxon *Heliand,* retells the life of Christ; and in both England and the North Germanic area end rime is introduced long after the adoption of Christianity. If the introduction of Christianity influenced Germanic verse form, its influences must have been gradual and accompanied by other forces.

The period of change in verse form saw other changes than those in Germanic life. One of these is in the medium of poetry, the languages. Before and after 800 the various Germanic languages underwent marked changes, especially in

[1] W. Scherer, *Geschichte der deutschen litteratur* (5th ed., Berlin, 1889), 38–39.

5

their vocalic and syllabic systems. Another was change in the audience. The Germanic scop sang his ballads before the court of a chieftain, before the warriors in the hall. The monk Otfrid, on the other hand, owes the impetus for writing his epic especially to a woman, and while he composed his poem to be recited he was punctilious in the correction of his manuscript and sent copies to various clerical friends who could read them; no longer did the audience consist of warriors and no longer was a work transmitted solely by word of mouth. By 1200 the audience for poetry was again the court, but its make-up now differed considerably from that of a few centuries earlier. Just as the audience influenced the subject matter—the courtly audience of the thirteenth century preferred Celtic and Romance story to the Biblical stories of the earlier monks or the Germanic subject matter of their predecessors—so they must have affected poetic form. The linguistic changes, while more subtle in their influence, can hardly have been less powerful. All of these—the changes in language, the changes in audience and presentation, the changes in direction of influence—require further study, both in their single and in their combined effects on Germanic verse form.

The poetry that has come down to us is adequate to demonstrate these changes in form, even though we have only a small proportion of that originally extant in the early periods. From the continent very little alliterative poetry remains, but enough to assure us that it had flourished here as well as in England and the north. When we avoid the traditional regional groupings into Old Norse, Old English, Old Saxon, and Old High German, which are based on linguistic rather than literary differences, and look on Germanic poetry as a whole, we find a considerable variety in both old and new forms and a variety in content and excellence.

The thesis that all works written in the Germanic languages until about the year 1170 belong to one tradition, that they make up Germanic literature rather than individual national literatures, can be supported by examination of the various pieces and genres of which evidence has come down to us. Specific charms, like that surviving in a manuscript in the German town of Merseburg, probably differ little from the charms employed in the time of Caesar and Tacitus.

Eiris sazun idisi,   sazun hera duoder.
Suma hapt heptidun,   suma heri lezidun,
suma clubodun   umbi cuoniouuidi :
insprinc haptbandun,   invar vigandun.
     Women once were sitting,   sitting one by one,
     some binding bonds,   some banning hosts,
     some chopping away   at chains and cuffs ;
     from your bondage go,   escape from the foe.

Similar charms in other Indo-European literatures, notably the Atharva-veda, support the suggestion that the form was general Germanic and that the Germanic and other speakers of Indo-European languages had preserved this form from their common Indo-European heritage of as early as 2000 B.C.

The general Germanic literature of the first centuries of our era was also much richer than the scanty remains suggest. We can ascribe forms other than the charms to the common Germanic period. From episodes in the Old English and Old Saxon book epics we can conclude that these languages too had possessed ballads such as those surviving only in the north : the bard in *Beowulf* sings ballads in the hall of Heorot. Moreover, the northern ballad of Weland the Smith has its home in Old Saxon territory; the scop of the Old English *Widsith,* who gives an excellent, if idealized, account of the extent of a storyteller's wanderings, was born in northern Germany. By comparing relatively old works such as the *Hildebrandslied* in Old High German and the *Fight at Finnsburg* in Old English with Old Norse poems, we can arrive at

7

a picture of alliterative poetry as it was before the influence of the Latin book epics, that is, a picture of the general Germanic poetry.

We may assume that just as the Germanic tribes once spoke one language, so they used one verse form; although we owe to Iceland our best specimens of it, we know that the Icelanders merely preserved and developed what they had brought from Norway, where, as the sagas tell us, taste for the form had not vanished though the native works had. That poetry in this form flourished not only among the North Germanic peoples and their West Germanic neighbors in England and on the continent but also among the East Germanic group we have by report from Jordanes, who states that the Goths in early times celebrated the deeds of their ancestors in song.[2] And that our best extant specimens of Germanic verse form were preserved on Iceland is due to the island's history; here the Germanic literature was not identified with paganism when this finally bowed peacefully to Christianity but was maintained for amusement, as was Homer among the Greeks; nor were precious manuscripts lost in subsequent wars.

Although most of these common Germanic forms persisted as late as the thirteenth century, long after the various Germanic peoples had established discrete homes, the separate groups had by this time developed some new and individual forms. The North Germanic peoples who settled Iceland had perfected the prose saga, a form totally unknown among the Germanic peoples living in the area of present-day Germany; the Germans on the other hand had taken over French forms such as the dawn song and the courtly epic which were not cultivated by Icelanders. By 1200 even native Germanic forms had developed in entirely different ways: the song of praise had become a terse, stylized ode among the Icelanders; among

---

[2] *Romana et getica, Monumenta Germaniae historica,* Auctorum Antiquissimorum, ed. Th. Mommsen (Berlin, 1882), V, 1, 65.

the German poets its successor was put into the tripartite mold taken over from France.

For later times our knowledge of Germanic literature is not dependent on inferences drawn from chance survivals, like the *Beowulf,* on literary references, or on the conclusions of scholars, but everywhere we find numerous examples of the various forms. Though we might wish for fuller records from the early periods, it is not lack of material which has prevented a study of the changes in Germanic verse form.

The lack of such study seems rather to be a result of the curious reluctance that writers and literary scholars exhibit to analyze language. Other literary studies abound—historical, sociological, and biographical—but when attention is turned to the language of poetry, it proceeds no farther than work on meaning, or semantics, and versification. To be sure, one finds discussions on the rhythms of language, but these are impressionistic. In his section dealing with modern English poetic form, Gardner defines Hopkins' innovations in terms of versification, saying that "Sprung Rhythm . . . is virtually a stress-metre derived from a number of sources, literary and otherwise."[3] Only as an afterthought does he add: "Sprung Rhythm, moreover, is closely akin to the rhythms of ordinary speech." But these he does not attempt to define. The bases of poetic rhythm and the "rhythms of ordinary speech" are clearly the duration of sound-classes, their distribution, the structure of groups of sounds, the type and location of accent, whether it consist of variations in pitch or intensity, and what the degrees of these may be. Linguistics provides us with data concerning these. It remains to apply such data to the study of poetry.

Study of changes in Germanic poetic form may yield other results than an improved understanding of the aims of

[3] William H. Gardner, *Gerard Manley Hopkins* (2 vols., London, 1944–49), I, 42.

the successive generations of Germanic poets. It may not be uninstructive for an understanding of changes in poetic form today. Like early Germanic poetry, current Germanic, especially English, poetry has been undergoing changes in form, though even in Hopkins the changes have not been so extensive as those a thousand years earlier. But they are being effected by self-conscious artists who attempt to define the influences on poetic rhythm. Eliot, for example, discusses these influences in his lecture *The Music of Poetry,* and he finds more important than the influence of past periods or foreign literatures the "natural law" that "poetry may not stray too far from the ordinary everyday language."[4] He ascribes the decline of English blank verse to disregard of this "law." But until we are provided with a comparison of the speech rhythms at the time blank verse flourished in England with those prevailing when blank verse became artificial, and their relation to the rhythms of blank verse, we are left with a statement of opinion, however interesting. Later in his lecture, Eliot returns to the dominance of speech rhythms over poetic form with the sentence: "And a language is always changing; its developments in vocabulary, in syntax, pronunciation and intonation—even, in the long run, its deterioration —must be accepted by the poet and made the best of." Again the actual basis of language rhythms—the phonological structure of a language—is skirted; but this statement, like the one cited above, is valuable for its awareness of the sway of language, and language in change (which one may assume is what a classicist like Eliot means by deterioration), over a poet. One looks forward to an analysis of Eliot's speech, of the speech of his contemporaries in the changed linguistic surroundings, the speech of his predecessors, and to comparisons of them and study of the interrelationships between the

[4] T. S. Eliot, *The Music of Poetry* (Glasgow, Jackson, Son & Co., 1942), 13.

changes in speech and those in poetic form. Until such burdensome tasks are completed the older periods of the language and literature, which have been minutely studied, will permit us to recognize more clearly parallelisms between literary and linguistic changes.

Not all the innovators in modern English poetic form share Eliot's preoccupation with a return to the spoken language. Pound's innovations consist much more in the importation of new forms, primarily from Provençal poetry but also from Oriental and older Germanic verse. Hopkins was particularly concerned with change in presentation; his poems were to be read aloud, not merely with the eye. Hopkins himself found them unpalatable when read silently.

These three influences—the spoken language, imported forms, and oral presentation—are those predominant in the changes introduced into modern English poetry; they have interpenetrated one another, though associated with the personalities and the subject matter of their proponents. Provençal motives and forms, like the Villonaud, can hardly be dissociated today from Ezra Pound. Yet in general, as in the contemporary search for a new dramatic form, we find the three influences variously at work: Fry is molding conversational speech rhythms into dramatic verse; O'Neill attempted to introduce the classical drama form into English while using colloquial speech.

In older Germanic poetry we find the same three influences. There, possibly because of the perspective of time, they are more easily dissociated. Germanic poetry, therefore, despite losses and difficulties of interpretation owing to transmission, has various advantages over contemporary poetry for the study of change in verse form. The characteristic innovation in Middle High German poetry, and medieval Germanic poetry in general, is the introduction of the Provençal verse form; the tripartite stanza of Provençal poetry, for example, was brought into Middle High German through direct imitation of Provençal models. The characteristic innovation in late Old English and Old High German was the attention to written poetry; Otfrid, for example, sent a copy of his poem to Bishop Solomon with the hope that he therein would find something worth reading (*Ad. Sal. 7*) :

Oba ir findet iawiht thes,   thaz wirdig ist thes lesannes :

We have no statement like Eliot's from which we can infer a preoccupation of any Germanic poet with the rhythms of contemporary speech, but comparison of the *Heliand* with Old English poetry is adequate to demonstrate the *Heliand* poet's use of colloquial rather than traditional patterns. Germanic poetic form then, like modern English poetic form, underwent changes, some of which can be related to linguistic changes, others to changes in presentation and audience, and still others to changes in foreign influences.

In the poetry of the older period such innovations are not as intimately bound up with the poet's personality and the subject matter as in modern verse. When reading earlier Germanic verse, therefore, we can direct our attention to the poetry itself without regard to the person of the poet, for in this society authors did not obtrude their personality on the audience. Only by exception do we even learn their names. The saga of Egil, possibly the most eminent Old Icelandic poet, tells us of him as one of the most vigorous northern fighters; almost incidentally we learn to know poems which he composed at dramatic moments, such as his "Life-ransom" of 937, or those which illustrate his vigorous personality, such as the "Lament for his Sons." To be sure, the Old High German monk Otfrid wrote three prefaces and a postscript to his epic, in the last of which he embedded his name, but only to gain the prayers of others and to honor his countrymen, who alone had no adequate presentation of the life of Christ in their tongue; his poem bears as little individual stamp as does its anonymous Old Saxon predecessor, the *Heliand*. Absence of biographical detail in poetic works may not, of course, coincide with lack of individual stamp, as is clear from Shakespeare. But the whole atmosphere in Germanic society opposed arbitrary innovations by the poet. Two accounts, perhaps intended as critical introductions, of early Germanic poets have come down to us: the well-known one of Bede about Caedmon; another about the author of the *Heliand*. Both dwell so much on the personality of the poet that they give us no biographical information we should consider important: the birthplace of the poet, his education, and his occupation, whether cleric or layman. Our fanciful ancestors preferred to use up their precious parchment in depicting each poet as an unlettered shepherd who was inspired in a dream. Although much information that we seek about authors has been drawn from these accounts, it cannot be received with assurance, for both accounts are idealized in the tradition of their day. Louise Pound has even found parallel accounts in American Indian and Australian poetry, on the basis of which she associated them "with the dream-lore and poetry of all ages."[5] Since the Germanic audience put their poets in an idealized atmosphere, it is highly unlikely that they could have modified at will their inherited forms. Rather, all of our evidence indicates that the Germanic poets were completely traditional in form.

The difficulties of an individualistic poet, even centuries after the introduction of Christian culture with its emphasis on the individual and devotion to individual writers like Vergil and Ovid, are apparent in contemporary criticism of Wolfram von Eschenbach. Wolfram's invention of new turns in

[5] Louise Pound, "Caedmon's Dream Song," *Studies in English Philology, A Miscellany in Honor of Frederick Klaeber,* ed. Kemp Malone et al. (Minneapolis, 1929), 232–39.

his story, as well as his obscure words and difficult syntax, drew scathing criticism from his contemporary Gottfried von Strassburg. For his deviation from the literary practice of the day, from adapting French epic story to German, Wolfram in his *Parzival* even had to resort to claiming a source, Kyot. Whether Kyot was Wolfram's invention or an obscure poet of whom no other record remains is beside the point here. To avoid censure for individualistic treatment of a story, Wolfram had to justify his departures from Chretien by ascribing them to a particular source. With such absence of individual stamp and submergence of the individual poet in tradition we can trace more fully the external forces modifying poetic form: the changes in language, the change in audience, and the impact of non-Germanic forms.

Study of the changes in form is further simplified by the maintenance of subject matter through such changes. While many new ideas and subjects, especially of Christian and Celtic origin, are found only in later Germanic verse, the older subjects were not abandoned. The legend of Hildebrand has survived both in Old High German alliterative verse and in late Middle German end-riming verse. Walther von der Vogelweide's song in praise of Landgraf Hermann[6] is in the same vein as the Old High German *Ludwigslied,* and this, like the Old Norse Skaldic poems, is a song of praise. The Nibelungen story was sung in various northern ballads— some of which exhibit the oldest features of alliterative form —but found its definitive treatment in Middle High German stanzas, whose rimes are virtually as pure as those of the most scrupulous courtly poets. Better control of a topic in literary investigation could scarcely be found.

Moreover, stylistic similarities are maintained. The fondness for paired expressions like Old Norse *sandr né sǽr* 'sand

---

[6] *Die Gedichte Walthers von der Vogelweide,* ed. Carl von Kraus (10th ed., Berlin and Leipzig, 1936), 35.7, 47.

nor seas', the Old High German *selida ana sorgun* 'solace without sorrows' has persisted through all formal change, even to Chaucer's *mayn and might* and modern English *might and main*. Both the early and late poets are fond of understatement. Hagen's reply to the invitation of the Huns in the Middle High German *Nibelungenlied* indicates the fate of the Burgundians in the oblique manner that the early Germanic poets preferred, stanza 1461:

"Nu lât iuch niht betriegen,"   sprach Hagene, "swes si jehen,
die boten von den Hiunen.   welt ir Kriemhilde sehen,
ir muget dâ wol verliesen   die êre und ouch den lîp:
jâ ist vil lancræche   des künic Etzelen wîp."
    "Be wary now," said Hagen,   "whate'er their promise be,
    those Hunnish messengers.   If Kriemhild you would see
    there you will surely forfeit   your honor as well as life;
    implacable in revenge   is King Attila's wife."

Equally persistent is the feeling of doom and revenge; it pervades the Middle High German *Nibelungenlied* and the late northern Hamlet tale no less than the Old Norse *Song of Weland*. Therefore, in studying the changes in Germanic verse form we are not faced with elusive differences that are marked in the poetry of other periods.

In so far as the changes in Germanic verse form have been noted they have been correlated with such external differences as are generally assumed to influence poetic form, especially with the introduction of new material. To be sure we find a subtle interplay between innovations in form and matter, especially around the periods of the most striking formal changes. The abandonment of the Germanic verse form follows the introduction of Christianity. The tightening of the North Germanic form follows upon contact with the Celts. The adoption of the Provençal lyric forms accompanies the cult of courtly love. Importations seem to account admirably in each of these instances for the changes in form. But we have already noted the absence of precise correlations between new form and matter. Alliterative verse was maintained in England, apparently in unbroken tradition, at least six centuries after the introduction of Christianity. Rimed verse, the characteristic form of Christianity, on the other hand, was written in North Germanic during the period of heathendom. Nor did courtly ideas succeed in dislodging the old forms in the north; some of the conventions of courtly love penetrated Icelandic verse and prose relatively early with no effect on the form. The correlations between changes in matter and changes in Germanic poetic form are therefore very, very general. None of the cultural influences accounts for the successful adoption of any of the new forms.

Relationships between the changes in poetic form and language have not escaped notice, but more than a superficial connection has been denied on a priori reasoning. For tyranny of language over poetic form and subject has seemed like a tyranny of inert material over creative force. Wider study of language, however, has shown in greater perspective that the tyranny of language can scarcely be overestimated: thought patterns are quite subservient to linguistic patterns. Thus Whorf found among the Hopi Indians a view of time relationships that contrasts markedly with those in western European languages and western European civilization, but is wholly bound up with the Hopi linguistic patterns.[7] The Hopi never have objectified time as have the European peoples; for them time is a separate dimension, so that they cannot speak of "four days" in the same manner as of "four chairs." Instead, their language demands a conception of time that agrees strikingly with that of modern physics. Only after centuries of work have European scholars been able to break through the

[7] Benjamin Lee Whorf, *Collected Papers on Metalinguistics,* Foreign Service Institute, Department of State (Washington, 1952). See especially "The Relation of Habitual Thought and Behavior to Language," 27–45.

time patterns imposed on them by their languages. Nor are these patterns fixed. Our habit of objectifying time, of counting days, hours, etc., like chairs and other objects, seems to have been acquired by Latin some centuries before our era, and probably somewhat later by the other western European languages. Europeans in the past have rarely studied languages outside this sphere, and these patterns have, therefore, seemed universal, especially since the grammar of other languages had been presented in terms of the western European system.

One does not have to look to American Indian languages to find limitations in the western European linguistic systems; they are readily apparent by comparison with other languages and cultures as well. Just as the European languages imposed on their speakers a peculiar view of time, so Europeans find it impossible to view other natural objects differently from the arrangement of such in their languages, for example, to visualize a world whose objects lack number. Nouns in the area of Chinese culture are neither singular nor plural, nor can they be. *Hitó* in Japanese refers to the concept of man, not to one man, men, or the man. The European languages are equally at odds with Japanese in pointing out individual human beings; Europeans use personal pronouns, words almost as objective—one might say impersonal—as any in the language. Reference to individuals in Japanese is impossible without concomitant ranking: *bóku* 'I' suggests inferiority, *watakusi* 'I' equality, and so on; one can most nearly approximate the European "impersonal" reference by use of the verb form, e.g., *mimásita* '(I) saw', which can, however, also mean 'he, you, they, etc., saw'. Conversely Europeans cannot convey simply the meaning of such words as *bóku* and *watakusi,* which are found in languages with systems of honorifics, even when such words are used in their most literal sense; when irony is introduced, when a word suggesting elevation is ap-

17

plied to an obvious inferior, one despairs of translation, though this is supplemented by footnotes. Linguists have scarcely begun investigation of such linguistic patterns and their influence on culture, and no work at all is available for their influence on poetry. Such "archetypal studies" of poetic imagery as have been made do not venture beyond the European languages, and scarcely beyond those of modern times; yet the word "archetypal" applied to so limited an area seems presumptuous. To merit the title, archetypal studies might at least penetrate beyond the European linguistic provinces.

But even without such studies it is clear that authors writing in the European languages are circumscribed in their subject matter and form. In learning their several languages they had not only their universe limited for them but also the possibilities of expressing this limitation. While infants in any linguistic area can utter an almost infinite variety of sounds, their elders are severely limited in the number of sounds they can use in speech; the process of language-learning involves loss of the ability to produce certain sounds as well as mastery of a very limited number. Thus a speaker of English has great difficulty acquiring and using the essentially simple nasal vowels of French; a speaker of any European language finds it virtually impossible to produce the pharyngeal sounds of Arabic languages. And what is more to the point here, an author cannot introduce foreign sounds in his material with any expectation that they will be pronounced differently from his and his audience's native sounds. He is strictly limited within the bounds of an already limited sound system. Neither in sounds nor in their method of production—their length, intensity, and pitch—can he exceed the patterns of normal speech. It follows that as this system changes, as it expands or contracts, so must his poetic repertoire. But although linguists have described the sound systems of various languages and times, and metrists the poetic systems, and although both systems change, the correlation of these changes has not been studied.

Some linguistic changes may effect changes in the ordering of the material world; after the verb system of the Germanic languages came to mark tense relationships rather than aspects, all actions were classed by time of occurrence, for example, whether they were past, future, etc., rather than whether complete, incomplete, and so on. The aspects of Biblical Greek now had to be expressed in compound-tense forms when translated. Some may affect poetic form; these very Germanic compound tenses introduced a great many weakly accented syllables in the line. It may be difficult to decide which of several possible causes may have influenced changes in poetic form. In investigating the relationships between linguistic and poetic changes we can assume a causal effect of language on poetic form if linguistic developments lead to a form of language that parallels the requirements of new poetic forms.

A poet must deal with two external forms: the form of contemporary poetry as well as that imposed on him by his language. Both limit him; the form of the language he writes in represents but a selection from the possibilities of human speech, and poetic form selects further patterns from any given language. Linguistic form restricts both his rhythmic and his semantic effects. It is as impossible to import the music of Chinese into English as it is the connotations of the Chinese language. When as in *Pisan Canto* 77 Pound inserts *chung* in his poetry, his English reader has no way of knowing its pitch accent, or more of its meaning than Pound himself tells him. The reader, not finding the segment *chung* in English, might pronounce it like the first syllable of the place name Chungking, or possibly, if he had read statements about Chinese transcription, like the first syllable of "jungle," and draw little more meaning from *chung* than from the first syllable of these words. But we do not need to go as far from English as Chinese; material inserted from within the group of Indo-European languages has no better fate. The footnotes to *The Waste Land* illustrate the difficulty an English reader experiences with *datta, dayadhvam, damyata,* and when one discusses the poem with even a select audience, it is clear that the simple German lines that Eliot quotes are equally obscure. Both represent a quaint interruption in rhythm and meaning, not a penetration beyond the English linguistic and meaning system. Eliot's very transcription of the Sanskrit words illustrates his adaptation of them to the English linguistic pattern —*dayadhvam* for *dayadhvām*—not to speak of the pronunciation of the reader who has no ready access to Sanskrit.

Only poets writing for a select and sophisticated audience attempt, like Pound and Eliot, to break through the limits imposed by their language. They rarely disregard the formal limitations imposed by contemporary poetry. Schools of poetry that, like the modern English vers libre group, assume that poetic form imposes no limitations are apparently rare, and short-lived. To illustrate the observance of poetic limitations we may note that contemporary English dramatists observe the formal restrictions traditional on the English stage rather than those traditional in Japan though many Japanese no dramas have now been translated into English. Poets, then, are generally aware of the limitations imposed by poetry, but they are usually quite unaware of the limitations imposed by language, as have been literary critics and linguists. We shall presumably continue in this blithe state until the language rhythms are described and their modifications in poetry investigated. Since even a description of the rhythms of such a highly investigated language as English is still fragmentary, investigations into the relation between poetic and linguistic rhythms have ample scope for development.

On the more complicated questions there have been

20

merely speculations; such is the successful adaptation of new forms. Why should the Provençal lyric form have yielded so readily to adaptation in Middle High German, and not at all in Icelandic, though we have evidence of a high poetic skill in Iceland before and after 1200 but evidence for quite the contrary in Germany before 1170? Hulme's suggestion of a correlation between new poetic forms and excellence of poetry is surely too simple.[8] Hazardous also is the assumption that we have no excellent Icelandic literature in the new form because the energies of gifted Icelanders were consumed in the political difficulties of the thirteenth and fourteenth centuries. There is little hope of solving this or even less complex problems by other than analytic methods. The poetry of any two subsequent periods involving change must be analyzed for single influences: language changes, demands of the audience, importations, and a striking poetic personality. But before any such analyses can be successful we must be aware of the forms themselves, both poetic and linguistic. Only after a wide variety of poetry has been thus investigated—poetry with different rhythmic bases from those of the Germanic languages (such as Chinese, Eskimo, and Arabic poetry), as well as specific periods (such as English poetry between 1750 and 1780), and specific authors (such as Milton and Goethe)—will we be able to understand the external processes of poetic creation, and possibly clear the way for an understanding of the human achievement called poetry. Apart from random observations we have only the last kind of study.[9] Inasmuch as tremendous energy has been expended in investigations of the early Germanic languages and their poetry, it may not be

[8] For this suggestion see his "Lecture on Modern Poetry," which is published in Appendix II of *T. E. Hulme,* by Michael Roberts (London, Faber & Faber Ltd., 1938); note especially 260.

[9] An example is Elizabeth Karg-Gasterstädt's *Zur Entstehungsgeschichte des Parzival* (Halle, 1925), in which she investigates the rhythms in Wolfram von Eschenbach's verse.

21

wholly inappropriate to undertake here a more comprehensive investigation in the change of poetic form.

The salient changes and developments in Germanic poetic form will be outlined in the following chapter. After the changes in form are clear, we will be able to compare them with other pertinent changes in Germanic culture and attempt to relate them, or show absence of relation.

Possibly the most important culture change is the development in the structure of the Germanic literary languages. Pertinent facts about the structure of the various languages will be given in the third chapter, compared with the structure of Proto-Germanic, the language from which they originated, and then related to the various changes in poetic form. Although the interrelationships here are most complex, the facts can be arrived at with relative ease and presented for the several literatures because the changes in linguistic structure are possibly those elements of Germanic cultural development that have been most carefully investigated.

While these linguistic changes were taking place, some bringing about prosodic patterns foreign to those of earlier poetry, others leaving the established prosodic patterns unchanged, the audience for literature was also changing. The bearers of Germanic culture varied from the warrior class to the clerical to the courtly, some of whom sought a written, others an oral, literature, at times accompanied by music, at times not. Changes induced by shifts in audience and presentation will be discussed in the fourth chapter, for, since they involve larger segments of form, they are susceptible of analysis only after analyses of linguistic changes.

The changes occasioned by outside influences affected particularly the largest segments of form, and will be discussed in the fifth chapter. In the Conclusion an attempt will be made to evaluate the changes in Germanic literary form and to interrelate the influences by which they were produced.

2 THE OLD GERMANIC VERSE FORM

Alliterative poetry was maintained to various points of time in the several Germanic languages. The date of its abandonment correlates with the geographical location of the language areas. In Old High German, the southernmost of the Germanic dialects from which literary material has survived, it was abandoned in the middle of the ninth century; in Old Icelandic, the northernmost, it was abandoned only in the thirteenth century, and then not entirely, for here the new form has retained elements of the old. The other Germanic languages in which poetry has been transmitted to us, Old Saxon and Old English, adopted the new form between these dates. Whatever documents have come down to us in other Germanic dialects, Gothic, Old Frisian, and Old Franconian, owe their importance to linguistic, rather than literary, criteria. For Old Saxon, the language spoken in northern Germany, the date of abandonment is uncertain because no poetry has come down to us from later than the ninth century. Yet here the alliterative tradition was stronger than farther south, for a long alliterative epic, the *Heliand,* was composed in Old Saxon shortly before the Old High German monk Otfrid wrote the first Germanic epic in rimed verse.

In England, the alliterative form was in general use until the Norman Conquest; when English verse was resumed again after the interruption from the continent, the new form

23

had replaced the old, except in the north and west. Here there was a curious "revival" of the alliterative form in the thirteenth and fourteenth centuries, continuing into the sixteenth, which is difficult to explain unless we assume a continuous tradition. Even though the southern English poets do not make use of the alliterative form, it seems to have been widely known, for Chaucer was able to let the gentle parson plead inability to handle the verse form of the north with its "rum, ram, ruf" as well as the southern rime.[1] Much as the Middle English alliterative poems differ from the Old English, they contain some of the same characteristics, such as the use of nominal compounds, e.g., *faederhus* 'ancestral home'. Since these are not found in the Middle English literature written in the new form, the simplest explanation for their use is the assumption of a continuous tradition of alliterative verse.[2] The alliterative form may have survived in these very areas of England because of the powerful Scandinavian influence. Whatever the complex causes contributing to its survival, it was the north— the Scandinavian areas and northern Britain—that maintained alliterative poetry longest, the south that abandoned it earliest.

Although the structure of the alliterative line is parallel in all Germanic poetry, forms longer than the line differ characteristically in the north and south. The northern poetry is stanzaic, the southern stichic. The two forms may be compared with linguistic divisions and length of survival. The three southern languages—Old English, Old Saxon, and Old High German—belong to the West Germanic linguistic group, the northern to the North Germanic group. And though alliterative verse survived in northern England later

---

[1] See "The Parson's Prologue," *The Complete Works of Geoffrey Chaucer,* ed. Fred N. Robinson (Boston, Houghton Mifflin Company, 1933), 272.
[2] For a fuller discussion see J. P. Oakden, *Alliterative Poetry in Middle English* (Manchester, 1935), especially 113–68.

than the time of Chaucer, it apparently did not escape Scandinavian influence, being in part stanzaic, as in *Sir Gawain and the Green Knight*. We shall, therefore, speak of a northern and a southern type of Germanic alliterative poetry, characteristics of which will be discussed at greater length below.

In both areas the kinds of poetry are severely circumscribed. If we utilize the Aristotelian classification of literature—dramatic, lyric, and epic—we find native poetry resembling only the last. Even the use of this term in Aristotle's sense is difficult to justify by reason of both form and treatment. A favorite feature of the Germanic short epic was dramatic dialogue; for example, all of the *Hildebrandslied*, apart from the introduction and conclusion, consists of dialogue between father and son. Nor does the substance of the *Hildebrandslied* differ appreciably from that of a Greek drama. Hildebrand is involved in a tragic situation as inextricably as is Oedipus, though he has yet to perform his tragic act while Oedipus has performed his long before the opening of the drama. Despite this difference the interest in both works lies in the growing awareness of the protagonist that he is involved in a tragic situation and in his form of meeting it.

Nor is the lyric element absent in the Germanic epics as in Niðuð's lament for his sons:[3]

"Vaki ek ávalt,   vilia lauss,
sofna ek minnzt   síz mína sono dauða!
Kell mik í haufuð   kǫld ero mér ráð þín, . . ."
    "Ever wake I   woe bound
    Sleep flees from me   since my sons' death.
    Cold is my heart   cold was thy rede; . . ."

This and similar short lyric passages depict the feelings of

[3] The lines are taken from the Old Norse version of the *Song of Weland*, *Volundarkviða*, stanza 31, abbreviated *Vkv.* below; see *Edda*, ed. Gustav Neckel (Heidelberg, 1936), 118.

25

the characters, however, not those of the poet; accordingly the term *lyric* is only partially applicable.

Though we continue to use the term *epic,* in neither the northern nor the southern verse was there emphasis on narration until the long epic was introduced in the south on the pattern of Latin epic poetry. The Germanic audience already knew the stories. It was the task of the poet to depict the most dramatic incident in them, and its effect on the fate of the protagonists. Only in a modified sense may we, therefore, use the term *epic* to describe Germanic verse.

The types of poetry in the north and south are further limited by the choice of medium. In the north, prose became the vehicle for what might have become the longer epic, so that only the short ballad remained for poetry, apart from such genres as ritualistic, magical, and proverb poetry that Heusler calls the "lesser genres."[4] In the south, Latin was generally preferred over the native languages for personal expression, as in the hymns; only from England do we have more than one sporadic poem, such as *Deor's Lament,* which depicts the mood of the writer.

In the north, the surviving poetry consisted of ballads, some of which dealt with the story of a god or ancient hero, others with praise of some living personage. The former are anonymous; the latter were written for specific occasions by well-known poets. The anonymous ballads, known as "Eddic poetry" after a manuscript heading, present incidents from the stories of Germanic (not specifically North Germanic) gods and heroes. The occasional poetry, known as "Skaldic verse" after its writers, the skalds, deals with specific incidents in the life of the acquaintances of the author, usually with his chieftain, assuming for its poetic figures an intricate knowledge of Germanic mythology, but never providing such in-

[4] Andreas Heusler, *Die altgermanische Dichtung* (2d ed., Potsdam, 1941), 26–28, *passim.*

26

formation. Apart from the Eddic and Skaldic verse, and the "lesser genres," the northern literature was written in prose.

The south, on the other hand, maintained only enough of these genres to assure us that they were employed in common Germanic times. The Old High German *Hildebrandslied* and the Old English *Fight at Finnsburg* may be compared with the northern Eddic poems dealing with Germanic heroes; the Old High German *Ludwigslied* and the Old English *Maldon* with the Skaldic occasional poems. The preponderant genre in the south is the long epic. Most of these deal with Christian story—*Beowulf* is a notable exception—with the life of Christ, with Moses or other Biblical heroes, and with saints. Besides these, and a few short epics, some nonnarrative poems survive—especially in England—magical charms, the closely related riddles, and songs of grief. Many of these genres are pre-eminent too after the change in form; the Middle High German period is eminent on the one hand for long epics, on the other for short lyric poems dealing either with specific occasions (the *sprüche*) or personal emotions (the *minnesang* proper).

Though one characteristic line is used throughout the northern and southern alliterative poetry, we can detect definite patterns of development. The following lines from the various dialects all fulfill the "demand" of two stresses per half-line:

ON *Vkv.* 3.1   Sáto síðan   siau vetr at þat,
             Sat since   seven years thereafter

OE *Beo.* 2209   fīftig wintra   —wæs ðā frōd cyning,
             fifty winters   was then the wise king

OS *Hel.* 465   the habda at them uuîha sô filu   uuintro endi
                                              sumaro
             who had at that temple so many   of win-
                                      ters and summers

27

OHG *HL* 50   Ih wallōta sumaro enti wintro   sehstic ur lante
                    I wandered summers and winters   sixty
                                                        as exile

ME *Destruction of Sodom* 948   To wakan wederez so wylde
                                            þe wyndez he callez
                                            To wake weathers so wild
                                            the winds he calls

In other respects, however, these lines show characteristic differences. It is the purpose of this chapter to point out the main lines of development in the various areas from the time when poets who could write competent, or even excellent, verse in the common Germanic form to that when poets could handle as capably the new form with its poetic structure based on end rime and even rhythm. Before undertaking such a sketch we must determine what was the common Germanic form of alliterative poetry. How far back can we trace the Germanic alliterative line? If certain genres, such as the short epic, were already in use in Germanic times, did they follow the stanzaic form of the north or the stichic form of the south? Similarly we must note the stylistic and syntactic innovations in the various areas. After these problems have been discussed we will be able to sketch the changes in poetic form.

All of the oldest Germanic verse that has come down to us is alliterative. While none of this is older than the eighth century, we have runic inscriptions of the third and fourth centuries in the same form. Some of these were apparently intended as verse, and like the inscription on the famous horn of Gallehus:

Ek HlewagastiR HoltijaR   horna tawidō
    I Hlewagastir, the Holtijan,   the horn contrived.

follow the formal "demands" of an alliterative line: (1) The line is bound together by the alliterative *h*'s. (2) These occur

28

at the beginning of accented syllables. (3) The most important word from a metrical point of view occupies the first stress of the second half-line. We also find in this inscription the "freedoms" of the alliterative line: (1) The number of unaccented syllables is not restricted, varying from three with *Hle-* through two with *Holt-* to one with *horn-*. (2) Anacrusis is permitted before the first accented syllable. (3) The last accented syllable does not share the alliteration. Lines similar in pattern can be found in the later Germanic verse, for example (*HL* 3 and *Vkv.* 37.2):

Hiltibrant enti Haðubrant,   untar heriun tuēm;
   Hiltibrant and Haðubrant,   their two hosts between;
né ek þik vilia, Vǫlundr,   verr um níta
   nor I, Weland, might wish   worse to harm you.

We can therefore assume that the form of the alliterative line had been standardized five centuries before the surviving Germanic verse was first written down.

The earlier history of Germanic verse remains obscure. Unfortunately, Tacitus and Caesar neglected to preserve any specimens of the Germanic poetry they allude to. Tacitus' mention, in his *Germania,* Chapter 2, of the traditional grouping of the Germanic tribes into *Ingaevones,* (*H*)*erminones,* and *Istaevones* may preserve for us the accented sections of a verse with vocalic alliteration. If so, we may push our date backward several centuries to around the beginning of our era. But beyond this we can only make inferences, primarily on linguistic evidence.

From the structure of Germanic alliterative verse we can conclude that it did not exist before the Germanic accent shift. In the earlier stages of Germanic the accent was variable; this we know from Verner's demonstration that the interchange of consonants, maintained today in the English past-tense forms *was: were,* correlated with the variation of the Indo-

European accent, which also survived in Vedic Sanskrit.[5] At some unknown time before our era the accent in Germanic became fixed on the first syllable, and was characterized by strong stress. Alliterative verse on the Germanic pattern was impossible before this shift. Whether it was built on a type of verse that was inherited from the earlier period of Indo-European unity is mere speculation. The *gāyātri* rhythm of the Vedas, if also inherited in Germanic, could readily have been modified to the rhythms of the alliterative line after the change of stress; and alliteration is not unknown in the Vedas. Nor is there any inherent improbability in the theory that such a form could have been maintained to the time of the Germanic accent shift, a period as long as that during which alliterative verse and European rimed verse flourished. However fascinating such speculations may be, in the absence of any literary remains until the eighth century A.D., they remain highly fanciful.

For descriptions of general Germanic verse we have available no materials which permit us to describe segments longer than the alliterative line. For describing the alliterative line we have evidence like the Gallehus horn inscription. Though this was found in North Germanic territory it is so early—dating from before the completion of the Germanic migrations—that few linguistic changes had taken place which would separate its language from Proto-Germanic. And since the literary remains in the various Germanic dialects contain numerous lines like it, we can assume a continuous tradition for the single line.

But very little of the earliest Germanic verse is constructed as a series of lines. Two less simple forms were developed, one in the north, another in the south. In the north

[5] Formerly this was an interchange of voiceless spirants after accented syllables with voiced spirants before accented syllables; compare Old English *wearð* : *wurdon* 'became' with the Sanskrit forms *vavárta* : *vavṛtimá*, in which the position of the accent is indicated.

30

we find ballads composed of longer units, stanzas varying from two long lines to four, sometimes more. The southern poetry lacks such ballads, containing instead, besides alliterative epics patterned on Latin epic poetry, shorter poems of fifty to a hundred lines in which there are no regular metrical units longer than the alliterative line; such units as are found in these poems are determined by syntactic and stylistic rather than metrical grouping. Whether the general Germanic verse was composed in stanzas like the northern verse, or in irregular units like the southern, is again unclear.

At first approach it seems more attractive to consider the northern stanzaic ballads the Germanic form. Roman authors speak of Germanic song, a name apparently more applicable to the Old Norse ballads than to the West Germanic short heroic odes. And literary scholars, especially those of the nineteenth century, considered ballads the forerunners of epic verse. But this theory has more arguments against it than in its favor. In speaking of the Germanic song Tacitus singles out its irregularity (*clamor inconditus*). Throughout the Germanic territory we find a progression from irregularity towards regularity in form, in the Middle High German *Nibelungenlied* with its four-line stanzas but no less so in the Old Norse Eddic and Skaldic poetry. Moreover, those genres which, apart from the very short charms and similar folk poetry, are agreed to be oldest—the song of praise and the heroic ode—are the ones preserved in the West Germanic irregular form. Furthermore, when the bard in Heorot sings his ballads, in a "southern" poem to be sure, but one dealing with the northern area, the poet does not shift to the Old Norse stanza form. The evidence against considering the stanzaic form the more original is therefore stronger than that in favor of the form maintained in the south.

If we compare two of the oldest poems in both languages, the Old Norse *Song of Weland* and the Old English *Fight at Finnsburg,* we find in both an irregular grouping of lines, from which either the northern ballad or the southern epic forms could have developed. Neither of these poems has escaped the characteristic features of its area, possibly through later modification: the *Song of Weland* contains some stanzas of similar structure: the *Fight at Finnsburg* some lines with syntactic breaks at the caesura rather than at the end. Yet these features are not maintained consistently in either poem, and we may assume that if the homes of these poems had been interchanged so might also such features. With few modifications, such as those suggested below, the *Fight at Finnsburg* might have been written down as a stanzaic ballad, the *Song of Weland* as a short epic. We may conclude, then, that the form of Germanic verse is better preserved in a few of the oldest pieces in our West Germanic literature than in the northern ballads.

The *Fight at Finnsburg* may therefore illustrate for us the characteristic Germanic verse form. The poem begins as follows (2–12):

Hnæf hlēoþrode ðā heaþogeong cyning:
'Nē ðis ne dagað ēastan, nē hēr draca ne flēogeð,
nē hēr ðisse healle hornas ne byrnað;
ac hēr forþ berað, fugelas singað,
gylleð grǣghama, gūðwudu hlynneð,
scyld scefte oncwyð. Nū scȳneð þes mōna
waðol under wolcnum; nū ārīsað wēadǣda,
ðē ðisne folces nīð fremman willað.
Ac onwacnigeað nū, wīgend mīne,
habbað ēowre linda, hicgeaþ on ellen,
winnað on orde, wesað on mōde!'

  Hnaef counselled then king untried in war:
  "This is not dawn from the east, no dragon flying,
  nor here in this hall are the horns burning;
  but forth they are battling, birds are singing,
  resound the grey-coats, zoom the spears,
  shield to shaft answers. Now shines the moon

32

wandering under clouds;   now arise woe-deeds,
that the wrath of this troop   will arouse.
But awake now   warriors mine,
sieze your shields   show courage,
be first in the ranks,   faithful in mind."

An examination of these lines shows how little they are removed from the Germanic form. Almost every line might be independent, as are the individual lines of the oldest charms and the Old Norse ballads; line 9 alone is connected syntactically to the preceding line. Only lines 7 and 8 show the characteristic West Germanic form of the alliterative line with their enjambment, that is, syntactic breaks in the middle of the line rather than at the end. And here only do we find the stylistic device of variation—the repetition of a concept in different words—which with the syntactic device of enjambment was the innovation that distinguishes the southern poetry from the northern. Stylistically, then, these lines are out of keeping with the rest of the poem. The first half-line of 8 is a poetic description of the moon, adding no new material; and 7a too is little more than a varied form of 6b. If these half-lines were omitted the passage would approximate an Old Norse heroic ballad, with no loss in essential material. Half-line 7b would then stand as the first half-line to 8b, and to bring about alliteration the wēa- of 8b might be replaced by an element beginning with m, such as mān-. Omission of 8a would harm the passage little; Klaeber comments on it :[6] "A stereotyped expression is here put to a fine, picturesque use." Old Norse poetry and early West Germanic poetry rarely engage in such picturesque expressions. Half-line 7a, "shield to shaft answers," is a bit premature in the passage; wēadǣda 'dire deeds' is hardly more pertinent than māndǣda 'evil deeds.'

[6] Fr. Klaeber (ed.), *Beowulf and the Fight at Finnsburg* (3d ed., Boston, D. C. Heath and Company, 1936), 251.

33

By these modifications this is not suggested as an "earlier form" of the introduction of the *Fight at Finnsburg,* but is merely used to illustrate how little was the difference between the northern ballad form and the early southern heroic ode. The recomposed forms of ancient verse that one sometimes finds in handbooks, such as the Old Norse version of the alliterative lines on the Tune stone, may have some pedagogical value in linguistic studies, but for study of literary form they are as absurd as similar passages of Chaucer would be if one kept Chaucer's words but strained them through the sound laws.

With these changes this part of the *Fight at Finnsburg* would consist of two stanzas: the first dealing with the portents, visual and aural; the second, after a transition through a sensual image, with the actual situation. Unequal stanzas of eight and ten half-lines would be quite normal in such an early ballad, but if the poem had been transmitted in the northern tradition the second stanza might also have been reduced to eight half-lines through omission of the last two half-lines. That these omissions and changes are not wholly arbitrary, that they are based on the contrasts in style between such lines as 6 and 8, may be noted by comparison with the early West Germanic charms. There too we find symmetry of structure like that of lines 5*b*, 6*a*, 6*b*, and 11*b*, 12*a*, 12*b*, but no enjambment or variation; emotion is heightened by repetition of similar patterns as in the first Merseburg charm:

suma hapt heptidun,   suma heri lezidun,
suma clubodun . . .
        Some binding bonds,   some banning hosts,
        some chopping away . . .

The *Fight at Finnsburg,* as it stands, is a stylistic confusion between the older and newer forms.

Through such stylistic analysis we may detect in the

34

Fight at Finnsburg and the early heroic odes, such as the Old High German *Hildebrandslied,* the germs of two opposing tendencies, one of which was to take root in each of the Germanic areas: enjambment in the south, in the West Germanic area; strophic form in the north, in the North Germanic area. These contributed to making West Germanic alliterative poetry of the ninth and subsequent centuries so different from its contemporary North Germanic poetry. In the *Fight at Finnsburg* neither of these tendencies is carried through, or is even characteristic. Nor could one expect both to develop fully side by side. For enjambment is rare in any poetry with stanzas and lines as short as those in Old Norse. And only in highly sophisticated verse, such as Goethe's *Mailied* or Chaucer's *Troilus and Criseyde,* do we find a rigid stanza structure broken effectively by the emotion. In Germanic verse, too, there arose no balance between them. West Germanic poetry developed enjambment and variation, North Germanic poetry the stanza form and the *kenning,* a poetic compound consisting of two or more elements suggested by poetic fancy rather than by the context. In their extreme form, as in the Old Saxon *Heliand* and in some of the Skaldic poems, both literatures developed these tendencies to their utmost conclusion, and the conclusion of poetry.

But neither the northern nor the southern poetry ever broke through the stichic character of alliterative verse. Even in the most regular stanzas of the skalds and in the late Old English poetry, where syntactic pauses rarely coincide with rhythmic pauses, the characteristic unit remained the alliterative line. None of the gifted craftsmen who wrote in alliterative verse ever found a way of welding together successfully two successive lines.

An appreciation of Germanic rhythms requires only that the rhythms of the single line be understood. Though the Germanic poetic rhythms are based on those of prose and

35

though the rhythm of each individual line is therefore as-
certainable, in the over-all scheme of the Germanic alliterative
line there has been considerable dispute among scholars; for
the lines vary greatly in precisely those characteristics that
modern verse has standardized: the relative position of the
stresses and the number of unstressed syllables per line. Some
lines of the southern and northern poetry are quite similar in
structure, for example (*Beo.* 195 and *Vkv.* 25.1) :

gōd mid Gēatum,   Grendles dǣda ;
   good mongst the Geats,   Grendel's deeds ;
en ór augom   iarknasteina
   but from the eyes   ornate stones

others quite dissimilar (*Hel.* 1096 and *Háv.* 76.1) :

gibrengan uppan ênan berg then hôhon :   thar ina the balouuîso
   bring upon a mountain high :   where him the baleful one
Deyr fé,   deyia frændr,
   kine dies,   kinfolk die

But all have the same basic structure. This is built around
two characteristics : the alliterations and the stressed syllables.

   The principles governing choice of alliteration in Germanic poetry are clear, not only from the poetry itself but
also from a contemporary treatment, a treatise on it by a
master-poet, Snorri Sturluson. Every long line was divided
by a caesura into two parts, usually referred to as half-lines,
but these were bound together by the alliterations of at least
one of the two stressed syllables in each part. The important
alliteration fell on the first beat of the second half-line; it
determined the alliteration of the entire line, and only rarely,
virtually only in the Eddic verse, yielded this function to the
second beat of the second half-line. Apart from such rare lines
the second beat of the second half-line almost never shared
the alliteration. Both beats of the first half-line usually alliterated, as in the lines cited above; when not, the first more

commonly than the second (*Fight at Finnsburg* 5, 9, 10, 11, 12). The single consonants alliterated with each other—likewise the groups *sp, st, sk*—but any of the vowels could be associated. Throughout the whole area and time of Germanic verse these principles are observed with absolute consistency. Confronted by such regularity, scholars have been able to find problems only in extremely minor points, chiefly whether crossed alliteration, that is, alliteration of either the first or second stressed syllable in addition to the regular alliteration, as in the *Hávamál* line cited above, is deliberate or accidental.

The problems in the rhythm of the alliterative line, however, more than make up for the lack of them in alliteration. Here scholars have not attained even the uneasy agreement that is sometimes termed unanimity among them. For the characteristic rhythm is made up of two predominant elements—quantity and stress—which do not admit a simple relationship. There is no problem about the predominant elements of the line: these are four syllables, two in each half-line, which are elevated by stress, quantity, and two or three of them by alliteration. In these four syllables stress and quantity correlate, as does alliteration with the qualification stated above. Because of the interplay of stress and quantity, the term *lift* is used for the elevated syllables of Germanic verse, the term *drop* for the others. When, however, one attempts to set up a pattern for the nonpredominant syllables as well, the correlations ends. Scholars have accordingly selected either stress or quantity as the predominant characteristic and on this have built their metrical systems. Two systems stand pre-eminent among the many proposed: that of Sievers, and that of Heusler and Leonard. Each of these reflects the approach of its proponents toward poetry.

Sievers, whose approach to literary works was analytic, found five recurrent patterns of stress in the alliterative line and succeeded in classing all alliterative lines in one of these patterns or a slight variant. The patterns are as follows: / symbolizes chief stress, \ medial stress, x lack of stress, — a long syllable, ‿ a short syllable.

A $\acute{—}$x$\acute{—}$x
B x$\acute{—}$x$\acute{—}$
C x$\acute{—}$$\acute{—}$x
D $\acute{—}$ $\acute{—}$ $\grave{—}$x
E $\acute{—}$ $\grave{—}$x$\acute{—}$

All of them occur in *Beowulf* 7b to 10:

hē þæs frōfre gebād,		B
wēox under wolcnum weorðmyndum þāh,	A	E
oð þæt him æghwylc ymbsittendra	A	D
ofer hronrāde hȳran scolde,	C	A

solace for this he found;
he prospered on earth, with honors he throve,
until everyone of the areas round
beyond the whale-road should worship him.

The validity of these patterns was easily established in all areas of alliterative poetry, for they occurred with somewhat the same frequency in Old Norse as in Old English, some of them diminishing in frequency as the languages changed (D and E are less frequent in both Old Saxon and Middle English alliterative verse than in Old English). Furthermore, they were very useful in textual studies; many emendations of corruptions introduced in transmission were effected with their help. But the over-all irregularity in pattern displeased those students of Germanic poetry whose approach was literary rather than linguistic; the variety of unit patterns struck them as a metrical contradiction.

The attempts to find a consistent unit pattern in Germanic poetry are now associated with the work of two such scholars, although they had numerous predecessors: Heusler, a German literary historian, and Leonard, an American poet and scholar. They turned to the other predominant element of the Germanic alliterative line, quantity, and developed rhythmic systems based on time rather than on accent periods. If we let – represent a half note, x a quarter note, # a quarter rest, we would indicate Heusler's scansion of *Beowulf* 11 :

gomban gyldan ;   þæt wæs gōd cyning!
   tribute to pay ;   that was a true king!

$$\acute{-}\grave{x}\# \quad \acute{-}\grave{x}\# \qquad xx\acute{-}\#\# \quad \acute{x}x\#\#$$

By Sievers' system it would be scanned:

$$\acute{-}x \quad \acute{-}x \qquad xx\acute{-} \quad \acute{\smile}x$$

The systems based on quantity admit no variety in the unit patterns: all normal half-lines are made up of two feet or measures, and all feet were alike in time. Where Sievers had assumed a variation extending from one stressed syllable $\acute{-}$, to a stressed plus a medially stressed plus an unstressed $\acute{-}\_\grave{}x$, Heusler assumed equal measures, comparable to musical measures in 4/4 time. In Sievers' pattern $\acute{-}\_\grave{}x$, linguistic material would fill up Heusler's measure; in Sievers' pattern $\acute{-}$, however, the linguistic material, depending on its weight, might correspond to a whole note, or a half note, and to fill out the measure a half rest would be assumed. With the aid of a complex series of rules Heusler was able to fit all alliterative lines into his system.

   Systems so diverse naturally invited dispute among their adherents. Heusler's condemnation of Sievers stands or falls with his contention that poetry demands a recurrence of equal units. The adherents of Heusler maintained that Sievers' principles ruined Germanic verse as poetry, but upon admitting that Sievers himself read Germanic verse with feeling and understanding, declared that in his reading he failed to

39

follow his system. Sievers himself seems tacitly to have admitted this contention, for he never ceased attempting to find one underlying principle for Germanic verse. Whether such a basis for poetry is essential, is, however, open to question. So far as I know neither Sievers nor Heusler ever investigated the living poetry of non-Indo-European languages. To readers in the European tradition, some such poetry, for example, Eskimo, conveys an impression exactly like that Germanic poetry produced on Tacitus, of an irregular noise. There seems to be no recurrence whatsoever of like units. That modern Europeans look for these in current poetry does not preclude their absence in old Germanic verse; for whichever system of metrical analysis one adheres to, that of Sievers or Heusler, it is clear that an aesthetic revolution has intervened between old Germanic and current Germanic verse, and before this revolution no need may have been felt for recurrent equal units.

But, either with Sievers or with Heusler, we agree on the basic outline of the alliterative line. It contained four lifts, that is strongly stressed syllables whose quantity, either inherently or by resolution, was long. Anacrusis was common and was not limited to one syllable—the American metrist J. C. Pope, however, has attempted to fit even anacrusis into a set pattern, analyzing all lines of the *Beowulf* according to a 4/8 time pattern, in which the first measure may be heavy or light, but the second always is heavy.[7] Nor was the number of unstressed syllables per stress circumscribed. We can disagree only in the assignment of these, and the use of pauses. Unless one has firm aesthetic convictions, either arrangement, that of Sievers or Heusler, permits one to manage the Germanic line. Current favor rests with Heusler; but earlier scholars worked effectively with Sievers' system, and one has

[7] J. C. Pope, *The Rhythm of Beowulf* (New Haven, Yale University Press, 1942).

the feeling that it too would have been favored by at least one contemporary observer, Tacitus.

While the alliterative line remained basically unmodified in northern poetry, the southern epic introduced expanded lines, as in the passage cited here from *Beowulf*, 1166:

æt fōtum sæt frēan Scyldinga;   gehwylc hiora his ferhþe
                                    trēowde,
    sat at the feet of the master of the Scyldings;   each of
                            them his mind trusted,

Some scholars read expanded lines with two chief stresses per half-line, others with three. Expanded lines were employed chiefly in passages of strong emotion, and did not lead to a departure from the basic rigidity of Germanic verse form. The characteristics which determined the development of the alliterative line were linguistic and stylistic rather than metrical: a tendency to terseness in the north, to a free-flowing form in the south.

This terseness we find already in the oldest poems of the *Edda*, such as the *Song of Weland*. Yet even centuries of transmission through periods which insisted on a strict form were unable to obscure the freedom of rhythm in its lines. There is no question of rigidity, or syllable-counting; the pattern of accented and unaccented syllables differs from line to line, as does that of anacrusis. Irregular stanza structure suggests that such ballads had advanced but little beyond the form of the oldest Germanic poetry; and in the stylistic repetitions of stanza 33 we can easily see the pattern of the primitive charm.

Vkv. 31   "Vaki ek ávalt,   vilia lauss,
            sofna ek minnzt   síz mína sono dauða!
            Kell mik í haufuð,   kǫld ero mér ráð þín,
            vilnomk ek þess nú,   at ek við Vǫlund dœma."
    32   "Segðu mér þat, Vǫlundr,   vísi álfa:
            af heilom hvat varð   húnom mínom?"

33 "Eiða skaltu mér áðr   alla vinna,
at skips borði   ok at skialdar rǫnd,
at mars bógi   ok at mækis egg,
at þú kveliat   kván Vǫlundar
né brúði minni   at bana verðir,
þótt vér kván eigim,   þá er þér kunnið,
eða ióð eigim   innan hallar!"

31 "Ever wake I   woe bound
Sleep flees from me   since my sons' death.
Cold is my heart,   cold was thy rede;
would I this now,   with Weland to speak.

32 Tell me this, Weland,   wielder of Elves:
what fate befell   my fierce youths?"

33 "Oaths shall you first   all swear,
by the ship's deck,   and the shield's rim,
by the hip of the horse   and the hewing sword,
that you do not kill   the queen of Weland,
nor of my bride   be the bane,
though we have a wife   well-known to you,
or have an heir   inside your halls."

The treatment of matter in this and other Eddic poetry matches the terseness of form. Only the high points of the story are given; transitions from climax to climax and preparatory material are left to the hearer. The later Eddic poems maintain the terseness in form and matter, adding only a greater regularity in line and stanza.

Although the stanza structure of the *Song of Weland* is irregular, suggesting great antiquity (so that in the Old English rather than the Old Norse tradition it might have come down to us as a heroic ode), this poem like the later Eddic poems with more regular stanza structure contains the characteristic stylistic element of the northern verse, which was developed to the point of obscurity, the kenning. "Elf-ruler" of stanza 34, though transparent in meaning, fulfills the requirements for a kenning: it is made up of two elements; their meaning has no essential connection with the rest of the context. Kennings came to dominate northern verse, especially that of the skalds, so completely that it differed entirely from the West Germanic and the earlier general Germanic poetry.

Skaldic poetry developed in the north side-by-side with the Eddic verse, but in contrast with this was cultivated by the court poets, while the Eddic verse never lost popular favor. In Skaldic poetry we can observe the development in form that was already pointed out for northern verse, a development almost to the point of caricature towards formalism and rigidity. The oldest Skaldic verse, that of Bragi, is much less circumscribed in form than is that of its successors. The alliterative pattern of Eddic verse was maintained here, as always in Skaldic verse. Though syllabic regularity has been introduced, Bragi's rhythm is more irregular than that of the later Skaldic poets. And the other important innovation of Skaldic verse, internal rime, Bragi does not carry through with any regularity.

The first stanza of Bragi's *Ragnarsdrápa* reads:

Vilið Hrafnketill heyra,
  hvé hreingróit steini
Þrúðar skalk ok þengil
  þjófs iljablað leyfa.
    Wilt Hrafn-ketil harken,
      how the hue-bright of glow
    Thrud's shall I and thee, prince,
      thief's sole-blade praise offer.

Here already we see the Skaldic disregard of ease of content as opposed to form; the kenning *Þrúðar þjófs* standing for the giant Hrungnir, the further kenning "Hrungnir's (Thrud's thief's) sole-blade" standing for shield, and the rimes of *hrein-* with *stein-*, of *þjóf-* with *leyf-* are more important than a reasonably clear line. Furthermore, to achieve this pattern the syntax is askew; *skalk ok þengil* is wedged between two genitives. In prose, the content might have been expressed: "Hrafnketil, do you wish to hear how I shall praise the neatly-painted shield and the king?" The Skaldic departures from prose syntax and the rimes seem more foreign in Germanic verse than do the involved kennings; for kennings, though more simple, are found in all Germanic verse. But in Skaldic poetry alone do we find rime combined with alliteration as an essential structural feature. Moreover, the rimes and their patterns differ from those introduced later from Latin into Germanic poetry; they occur in syllables with chief or secondary accent, not in final syllables.

The Skaldic rimes were of two types: *skothendings* or incomplete rimes, e.g., *þjófs* : *leyfa, flaums* : *næma*, in which alone the final element of a syllable rimes; *aðalhendings* or complete rimes, e.g., *hrein-* : *steini, hildar* : *vildu*, which correspond in proportion of the word rimed to the rimes introduced into European poetry from the Latin. The incomplete rimes came to be regular for the odd half-lines, the complete for the even. End rime was found only sporadically, though oddly enough as early as Egil's *Hǫfuðlausn* of the tenth century. Cited here are the first four lines:

Vestr fórk of ver
  en ek Viðrís ber
munstrandar mar
  svá's mitt of far;
    Westward sailed we
      warding the sea
    of Odin's heart;
      you've heard my part.

Here, however, the two types of *hending* are not used.

Since Skaldic poetry observed a rigid stanzaic structure, abandoning the Germanic freedom of unaccented syllables though keeping the Germanic alliteration pattern, virtually the entire sound structure of the Skaldic alliterative lines was

44

determined by prosodic rules, especially in poems with end rime. In the first two long lines of Einarr skálaglamm Helgason's *Vellekla,* for example:

Hugstóran bið̄k heyra
  (heyr jarl Kvasis dreyra)
foldar vǫrð̄ á fyrð̄a
fjarð̄leggjar brim dreggjar.
    Oh lord, let now be heard,
      the lore of Kvasir's gore,
    fair words set forth, oh sire,
      the firth-men's song, earth-king.

the half-lines of which consist of six syllables, three syllables out of twelve have their initial sound determined by the alliteration, two their final consonants determined by *skothending,* two more their vowels and final consonants determined by *að̄alhending,* four syllables—*heyra, dreyra*—are determined by rime. The twelve syllables of these lines, therefore, are governed by eleven formal restrictions, the twelve of the next two long lines by seven; since the last syllable is always unaccented, the formal requirements must actually be accounted for in ten syllables. It is hard to see how anything in such poetry could have been appreciated but the cleverness of the poets; this stanza means: "I ask the land's courageous ward to hear my poem." And numerous incidents in the lives of the skalds illustrate their preference for linguistic sport rather than for ready understanding.[8] Jugglers were popular at other medieval courts, but none were as skillful with a storehouse of syllables as were the skalds.

The Skaldic formalism was not without effect on Eddic verse, chiefly in transmission; we find a progressively greater rigidity in stanza structure, and less fluctuation in the number of unstressed syllables, as in the tenth stanza of the *Valkyrialióð̄:*

[8] See L. M. Hollander, *The Skalds* (Princeton, 1947), 190–91, 203–205, 211, *passim.*

Vel kváðom vér   um konung ungan
  sigrhlióða fiǫlð;   syngiom heilar.
Enn hinn nemi, ˙ er heyri á,
  geirflióða hlióð   ok gumnom segi!
     Well chorus we   of the young king
       our lays of praise   auspicious chant.
     But he may take,   who hears us now,
       the spear-maid's song   and say it forth.

But apart from a development of these tendencies, North Germanic poetry introduced no thoroughgoing changes until influenced by Provençal poetry. To be sure, a variety of stanza structures was permitted, especially in Skaldic poetry. Eddic poetry was limited to two stanza forms: (1) the customary *fornyrðislag* of the stanza above, and a variant of it, the *málaháttr,* which contains more unaccented syllables, as in the first two lines of the *Song of Weland;* and (2) the *ljóða-háttr,* as in the *Hávamál 77*:

Deyr fé,   deyia frændr,
  deyr siálfr it sama;
ek veit einn,   at aldri deyr:
  dómr um dauðan hvern.
     Kine dies,   kinfolk die,
       dies just so the soul;
     this now I know   never dies:
       fame of former men.

In *ljóðaháttr* the alternate lines contain three lifts, occasionally but two. Larger forms made up of groups of stanzas were developed in Skaldic poetry, especially the *drápa* with its burden, reminding one somewhat of some of the Provençal forms. Yet even these complicated forms failed to break the bonds of the alliterative line; even in the *drápa,* alliteration circumscribed every line as rigidly as it had in the runic verse. Nor did the Skaldic rimes lead to larger units; inasmuch as rimes were constructed within the half-lines or the long line, they actually introduced a greater limitation on the poet than had been effected by the Germanic verse principles, making his largest unit a segment rarely longer than twelve syllables.

Even after the decline of Skaldic poetry, with the influence from Romance poetry, the units in the north were not much longer. The fourteenth-century *rímur* introduced a stanza pattern based on the Latin hymns, as in the following stanza from the *Filipo-rímur* I.29:

Tjáir þér eigi—tiggi kvað—
   at treysta mætti þínum;
ek má slá þik ofan í stað
   með einum fíngri mínum.
      Attempt not now, the king then said,
         to test that power of thine.
      I can tumble you on your head
         with any finger of mine.

But this was handicapped in development from the start by the formal trappings of Skaldic verse—alliteration and *hendings*—besides end rime, and it never equaled either the earlier Eddic or Skaldic verse, not to speak of the English and German verse based on the Romance patterns.

While the northern poets were exploiting the terseness inherent in the alliterative line, the southern poets were breaking through its stichic rigidity. In contrast to the northern poets, they extended the narrative possibilities of Germanic verse at the sacrifice of its form. For the chief device used in the south was enjambment, opposition between syntactic and metrical units. Metrical devices to link two or more alliterating lines are but sporadic, such as the use of the initial sound of the fourth stress for the alliterations of the next line, as in *Beowulf* 36–37:

mærne be mæste.   Þær wæs mādma fela
of feorwegum   frætwa gelæded;
      The mighty one at the mast.   There was many a fortune
      from far countries   furnished, as treasure;

47

or the repetition of alliterating sounds in two or more lines, as in *Beowulf* 1520–21 :

hildebille,   hond sweng ne oftēah,
þæt hire on hafelan   hringmǣl āgōl
                    (a mighty blow he gave)
     hewing with the battle-sword,   his hand did not slight the
                                       stroke,
    so that hewing on her head   the hissing sword sang
    (a fierce war-song).

Even though these devices may not be accidental they never succeeded in becoming a feature of Germanic poetry. Syntactic stops came to be characteristically located in the middle of the line. The early Old English poets used this device with moderation and effect; in *Beowulf* such breaks are found about once in every five lines. But later it was carried to an extreme : by the North German *Heliand* poet of the ninth century who even ended eighteen of his seventy-one fits in the middle of a line; and in England by the tenth-century *Judith* poet. The northern poets choked their alliterative poetry by packing too much material in the line; the southern poets, on the other hand, permitted it to dissolve in a torrent of words.

In the south, just as in the north, the poets developed a stylistic feature which enabled them to fulfill the requirements of their form; this probably contributed in turn to its trend of development. In the north, metaphors within metaphors enabled poets to convey to those initiates who could unravel the figure a wealth of material in the few syllables that their line granted them. The southern poets had no need to seek terse expressions, and such metaphors are almost entirely absent in much of their verse, especially that from the continent. Here, as in England too, the characteristic figure is the variation, an appositional construction restating previous material while introducing few or no new concepts but contributing to expansion. While the kenning is often obscure through terseness, the variation often contributes little besides words; through it the poet pulls his syntactic breaks to the middle of a line, as in lines 2413–14 of the *Heliand*:

Thô sâtun endi suîgodun   gesîðos Cristes,
uuordspâha uueros:
    There sat and were silent   the Savior's companions,
    those eloquent men:

Here "eloquent" is hardly more than inept. Like the northern kennings, the variations developed in complexity. Other arrangements are found besides the appositional, such as the chiastic, as in lines 1580–82 of the *Heliand*:

        Heliðos stôdun,
gumon umbi thana godes sunu   gerno suuîðo,
uueros an uuilleon: uuas im thero uuordo niut,
        The great men stood,
    the disciples about that Son of God   with no slight joy,
    the heroes all happy: they wished to hear those words,

Accordingly, syntactic and stylistic devices accompanied prosodic innovations in the south, as well as in the north, as the alliterative line was adapted to epic poetry. But in carrying these innovations to excess, the southern poets destroyed the external form of the alliterative line. To the same number of stressed syllables as are found in the northern verse, they added many unstressed syllables, both in anacrusis and between the stresses. The resultant lines are so padded that often the two alliterating stressed syllables fail to hold them up. That such expansion was due rather to attempts at development than inability to handle the form is clear from the "expanded lines." Such lines, containing half again as much speech material as the normal lines, are introduced in scenes of special dignity, as in some lines of the Sermon of the Mount in the *Heliand*, e.g., 1687:

Gerot gi simbla êrist thes godes rîkeas,   endi than duat aftar
                      them is gôdun uuercun,
    Keep ever your minds set on God's kingdom above all,
             and then do good works accordingly.

Under such a weight the Germanic alliterative line collapsed. The rhythm was built around two stresses per half-line in the south as in the north; yet one could scarcely imagine a greater difference than that between the southern (*Hel.* 1931*b*)

simbla sôkiad gi iu thene bezton sân
    always seek for yourselves the best straightway

and the northern (*Háv.* 77)

deyr fé
    kine dies.

The southern "expanded verses" may be the result of an attempt to extend the structure of the Germanic line—to proceed beyond the two central stresses, but if they were, the attempt was unsuccessful; even an additional stress could not support the extra material. Alliterative poetry in the south foundered under the weight of unstressed syllables.

    Revivals of the alliterative form were attempted in England, especially in areas under Scandinavian influence. Some of the Middle English poems, for example, *The Destruction of Troy,* have a more rigid form than the late Old English epics; of 14,044 lines, 13,999 have, according to Oakden, an alliterative pattern like that of the first line:[9]

Maistur in Magesté,   Maker of alle,

But even when the older Germanic patterns are kept, often the structure is merely external. Words that were unstressed in Old English, such as prepositions and even unimportant verbs like *is* and *are* may alliterate in Middle English; in other words the alliteration may vary from syllable to syllable, as in

    [9] Oakden, *Alliterative Poetry in Middle English,* 188.

50

Morte D'Arthur 3966 al*l*as, but 1153 al*las*. The alliterative form was apparently unable to support both the unaccented inflectional endings and the mass of function words, especially the articles and verbal auxiliaries, which had come into use in the Germanic languages after the eighth century.

Alliterative poetry was abandoned earliest on the continent. Despite the small amount of poetry that has survived from this area we have within fifty years an epic characterized by the extreme development of the alliterative form, the *Heliand* of about 830, and one in the new rimed form, Otfrid's *Krist* of about 860. The last alliterative Old High German poem that has survived, the *Muspilli,* was a contemporary of the *Krist;* whatever verse was produced in Germany after it is in the new form.

Otfrid, the author of the first epic in the new form, and presumably its originator, left no doubt about his revolution in form. In his preface to Liutbert he disclaims association with Germanic heathen poetry and points to Romans as his models: Vergil and Ovid in non-Christian story, and Prudentius, Arator, and Juvencus as his true forerunners. Moreover, he equipped his manuscript with accent marks that were to indicate his new rhythm. Form and rhythm are based on that of the Ambrosian hymn with rime, in the pattern it had developed by the ninth century. Compare the following lines of Otfrid, 1.2.7ff., with the Latin poem written by a contemporary.[10]

Joh íh biginne rédinon,   wio ér bigonda brédigon,
   thaz íh giwar si hárto   thero sínero worto;
Joh zéichan, thiu er déda tho,   thes wir bírun nu so fró,
   joh wío thiu selba héili   nu ist wórolti giméini.
     Yes, I begin to write again,   how he began to preach to
                            men,

[10] The Latin poem is taken from *Monumenta Germaniae historica poetae Latini aevi Carolini,* ed. Paul Winterfeld (Berlin, 1909), IV, 1, 137.

> that I be very much aware   of all of those his words;
> and wonders which he did then,   wherefore we may re-
>   joice again,
> and how the selfsame ransom   is now bestowed to all
>   mankind.

Odo princebs altissime   Regumque potentissime
Regale ceptrum suscipe   Longo regendum tempore.
> Odo, thou prince, highest of all,   Of kings too, most
>   potent of all,
> Your royal sceptre take and wear   And may you reign
>   forever and e'er.

Both of these poems have four stresses to the line, with the last falling on the final syllable. There are also characteristic differences. The Latin hymns have a fixed number of un-stressed syllables; even counting of syllables is quite general. Otfrid, on the other hand, may introduce more than one un-stressed syllable, in anacrusis or in the interior of a line. Be-cause of the structure of Latin the last stress of the line was filled by an inflected syllable; here Otfrid, like the Irish poets who adopted the Latin rimed form, permitted a stem syllable as well.

The resulting rhythm differed completely from that of alliterative verse. German scholars are fond of introducing musical notation to illustrate the difference, speaking of the new rhythm as 2/4 time, the old as 4/4. The metaphor may help to mark the difference despite its partial ineptness: but a metaphor is almost superfluous—the contrast stands out clearly when one compares any line of the older alliterative poetry, such as those of the *Beowulf* with the above, for ex-ample, 286:

Weard maþelode,   ðǣr on wicge sæt,
     The sentry said,   as he sat on his steed,

Never since, except by antiquarians, has the old rhythm been used in German verse.

Possibly because the transition from the old to the new form was most abrupt on the continent, the struggle to master it was here also longest and most painful. In England the change-over in form was gradual. Poems with Christian story continued to be written in England in alliterative form, though here too, as in Germany, Latin rimed hymns and epics were being composed. Their influence shows itself in the introduction of occasional rimes in Old English alliterative verse, as in Cynewulf's *Elene* 1236–50. Compare *Elene* 1250 with 1251:

> lēoðucræft onlēac,   þæs ic lustum brēac,
> willum in worlde.   Ic þæs wuldres trēowes
>   power of song diffused,   which with delight I used,
>   with joys in the world.   I of this winsome faith

In lines of the ninth century, like *Elene* 1250, rime is merely added to alliteration. In the *Anglo-Saxon Chronicle* of 1036, however, rime has attained the importance of alliteration, replacing it rather than simply accompanying it. For example:

> Ac Godwine hine þa gelette   and hine on hæft sette,
>   But Godwin him then let   and him in durance set.

In spite of Latin influence, alliterative verse in England survived generally to the time of the Norman invasion, and much later in the north and west, with a remarkable revival in the thirteenth and fourteenth centuries. In most of England, however, when English poetry was resumed after the Norman invasion, end rime and regular rhythm had replaced alliteration as it had earlier in Germany. Now the English began their struggle to gain command over the new rhythm and rimes. This struggle is possibly clearest in the works of Layamon, a contemporary it may be noted of the Middle High German poets who were masters of the new forms; we may find evidences of Layamon's struggles on almost every page, as in 27, 879–81:

53

And lette heom sone   senden to Rome,
and grette Rom-weren alle   mid græten ane huxe,
and seide þat he heom sende   þat gauel of his londe,
> And had them soon   sent down to Rome,
> and greet the Romans all   in greetings without taunts,
> and said that he them would send   the tribute of his land,

The first two of these lines fit the alliterative pattern; the very next introduces an alternating rhythm and rime in half-lines of four stresses, similar to the verses of *King Horn* which was written a short time later, about 1225, in rimed couplets, e.g. (9):

He hadde a sone þat het Horn,
Fairer ne miste non beo born,
Ne no rein vpon birine,
Ne sunne vpon bischine.
> He had a son whose name was Horn
> a fairer youth was never born
> nor by rain was rained upon
> nor by sun was shone upon.

Only greater artistry is needed to mold this rhythm and rime to that of the lyrics preserved from the same century, such as the well-known

Sumer is icumen in,
lhude sing cuccu!
Groweth sed, and bloweth med,
and springth the wude nu—
> Sing cuccu!

or *Alisoun*:

Betuene Mershe and Aueril
when spray beginneth to springe,
the lutel foul hath hire wyl
on hyre lud to synge.

In these lines we find no trace of the old forms.

The Old High German poet Otfrid is an even better

example than is Layamon to illustrate the difficulties occasioned by the introduction of the new form. The Old High German language provided Otfrid with a great deal of trouble, and only after writing a fair part of his poem could he manipulate it in the new form. In early parts of the poem he even perpetrated grammatical errors for the sake of his rimes, both in syntax and forms,[11] using, for example, as Baesecke pointed out, an unnatural order for his possessive adjective and a neuter ending on *lutentaz* instead of a masculine to obtain his rime (1.2.5)

Thaz ih lób thinaz   si lútentaz,
    That I the praise of thee   might expound free,

The rhythm in the earlier sections of the poem, parts of Books I and V, continue practices of alliterative poetry; some lines contain an excess number of unaccented syllables (I.3.10*a*) :

fon themo thie líuti, thes was nót,
    from whom the people, of this had need,

others, as *si lútentaz,* too few. A language fitted for the shifting rhythms of alliterative poetry required considerable experimentation before it could be used in the even rhythms that Otfrid was striving to imitate. That Otfrid was aware of the new rhythm even when he wrote his cruder lines we can assume from the existence of his patterns all around him in Latin verse, and his later success in manipulating the new form. For the last portions of his poem do not show unrestrained use of unaccented syllables or of anacrusis. Here the rhythmic scheme of the desired form has been achieved, to the point of dullness.

    Otfrid's achievements in rhythm were not passed on. The parochial Old High German monasteries seem to have

[11] See G. Ehrismann, *Geschichte der deutschen Literatur bis zum Ausgang des Mittelalters* (2d ed., München, 1932), I, 186.

been unable to transmit from monastery to monastery cultural attainments of any note, and since there was no one at Weissenburg to succeed Otfrid, no other monastery provided a successor. Whatever German verse was written between 870 and 1170 was, if anything, inferior to Otfrid's in mastery of rhythm. No poet of even Otfrid's limited eminence seems to have attempted to write German verse during these three hundred years. For whatever verse from this period has survived is as pedestrian in form as in content, as in *Ezzos gesang* 10 ff.

Duo wart geboren ein chint,
des elliu disiu lant sint,
demo dienet erde unte mere
unte elliu himelisciu here;
den sancta Maria gebar:
des scol si iemer lop haben,
wante si was muoter unte maget,
daz wart uns sit von ir gesaget;

> Then was born a child to us
> who all the earth holds in trust,
> him serves the sea, as well as lands,
> and also all the heavenly bands;
> whom the holy Mary bore:
> whence she'll be praised forevermore,
> since she was mother and a maid,
> that was to us about her said.

When one reads such verse, one wonders whether the monasteries employed their capable men in horticulture.

Only the great Middle High German poets gain mastery over poetic form, and over German rhythm. This is sudden, and complete. Possibly no German poet has achieved the grace and music of Gottfried, and his perfect command over form. His *Tristan und Îsolt* opens with the lines:

Gedæhte man ir zu guote niht,
von den der werlde guot geschiht,

sô wærez allez alse niht,
swaz guotez in der werlt geschiht.

> If those men were to count as nought,
> by whom good to the world is brought,
> then everything would be as nought,
> the good that to the world is brought.

The linguistic material here is under as complete control as in the greatest of the Skaldic poets, yet without forcing of the language and peculiar stylistic devices.

The struggles for control over end rime parallel those for control over rhythm. Otfrid's rime system, while the germ of that in Middle High German verse, seems crude beside it. And Otfrid has often been condemned for his rimes because of their unshapeliness. Such condemnation is not wholly just, for his technique here again was based on that of the Latin hymns, as especially Ludwig Wolff has pointed out.[12] In these only final inflectional syllables needed to rime, as *suscipe* : *tempore* of the poem cited (p. 52). But when rimes were taken over by the Irish, the different linguistic form brought about a different riming practice; since root syllables could occupy the fourth stress of the line, rime was no longer confined to inflection. Root syllables were rimed, both with one another and with inflected syllables, as in the Old Irish poem:

Messe ocus Pangur ban   cechtar nathar fria saindan
bith a menma-sam fri seilgg,   mu menma cein in saincheirdd.

> I and my dear Pangur white,   each of us had his delight;
> he prefers the mice to chase,   I my special field t'embrace.

Furthermore, as in the last rimes here, equivalence of consonants or even vowels in rime was not required. Instead, classes of consonants formed riming possibilities, such as the Old Irish class of stops: *c* (*gg, g*) *p* (*bb*) *t* (*dd*); under such rules *seilgg* and *-cheirdd* are good rimes. A second Old Irish

[12] *ZfdA,* 60 (1923), 265–83.

class was made up of the resonants and spirants, so that *l*, *r*, *m*, *n*, and such sounds as *f*, could rime, again as in *seilgg* and *-cheirdd*. Some Latin poets contemporary with, and others later than, Otfrid even rimed vowel classes, such as the three groups *i/e, a, o/u,* or classes determined by quantity, long vowels with long, short with short. Otfrid's rimes are much closer to the medieval patterns than are these.

Like the Irish poets, Otfrid strove for rimes greater in extent than the final inflectional syllables. Only the oldest parts of his poem contain unrimed lines, or lines in which only the inflected syllables rime (I.5.5, 15):

Floug er súnnan pad,   stérrono stráza,
    He flew the sun's path,   the street of the stars,
"Heil mágad zieri,   thíarna so scóni,
    Hail adorned maiden,   most beautiful virgin,

(Critics of Otfrid have not noted that few Latin poems before the eleventh century fail to contain some unrimed lines.) But even in the later parts we can detect some of his groping for a fuller rime. In one of his experiments to secure a fuller rime he attempted to construct rimes from the accented syllables, such as:

I.5.21   wiza : scinenta
V.14.10   noti : stozenti
V.15.12   dati : drageti
V.18.1   stuontun : luagetun

in which he disregarded everything that stood between the stem syllable and the inflectional syllable. Here, in addition to the inflected syllables which were adequate in Latin rime, the preceding consonants, e.g., *z* : *t, t* : *t,* and the vowels of the stem syllables were included in the rime. But his rimes on this pattern are relatively rare.

Most of Otfrid's rimes are pure, such as *min* : *thin, minan* : *thinan,* which include all of the word from the stem syllable on. When Otfrid did not use pure rimes, he attempted to rime at least the last consonant of the stem syllables. These are the rimes that were misunderstood until it was shown that Otfrid classed consonants in groups somewhat like the Irish poets. In this way *ziaro* : *thiorno* filled the rime pattern perfectly, as did

heili : gimeini   and   giburgun : wurbun
thanne : alle   huggen :·irzuken
heim : stein.

Again in riming, as in rhythm, there is deterioration rather than advance in the three following centuries. Poets observe a variety of conventions; some allowing themselves wide latitude in rime, others seem to be striving for pure rimes, but admit degrees of impure rimes that the poets with a higher percentage of impure rimes avoid. One poem of this time, Wernher's *Maria,* contains 30 per cent impure rimes, another only 15 per cent; but the latter, the *Linzer Entekrist,* permits impure rimes such as *widerwertic* : *dinc, cite* : *algeliche* that are not found in the *Maria.*[13]

Only after 1170 do we find careful attention paid to rimes, and again, as is the rhythm, so the rimes are meticulous. Even a popular epic like the *Nibelungenlied* observes high standards, for here too inexact rimes are avoided, though at the cost of variety. Middle High German riming standards are so high that whenever our manuscripts of the Middle High German poets present us with imperfect rimes, we accuse the transmission, not the poet, and emend the line.

In addition to the strictness in rhythm and rime, complicated stanza structures are introduced for the first time in German verse. Their elements may be illustrated by the first stanza of Walther von der Vogelweide's first poem in the

---

[13] For further examples see K. Wesle, *Frühmittelhochdeutsche Reimstudien* (Jena, Frommann, 1925), from which these data were taken.

small Heidelberg manuscript (the elements in parentheses are alternate forms introduced by scribes).[14]

So die bluomen uz dem(e) graze dringent,
sam(e) si lachent g(eg)en der spilden sunnen
in einem(e) meien an dem morgen vruo
   vnd die cleinen vogellin wol singent
in ir besten wise die si kvnnen
   waz wunne mac sich da genuozen zuo
   ez ist wol halb ein himelriche
svln wir sprechen waz sich dem(e) geliche
so sage ich waz mir dikke baz
in minen ovgen hat getan vnd tete och noch gesehe ich daz
     When the flowers from the grasses spring,
    as they were smiling at the playful sun,
    on any May day, early after dawn,
     and everywhere the little birds all sing
    such melodies that we must linger on—
    a greater joy I've never won.
     'Twere little more to taste of heavenly bliss,
    should we say what might compare to this?
    I'll tell you that which oft to me
    has seemed the best of earthly sights and would be still if
                e'er that I should see.

We note here the combination of strictness and freedom in form that is characteristic of Middle High German poetry, and apparently of all excellent verse, though with different degrees of application. The rimes are quite exact. The rhythm is even, and reproduced perfectly in matching lines, as 4 versus 1, 5 versus 2, 6 versus 3, etc. The stanza is divided into two equal subdivisions, stollen, of three lines, followed by a conclusion, *abgesang*. But apart from these observances the form is free: the type of rime, whether masculine or feminine is not prescribed; any number of stressed and unstressed syllables is permitted in any given line, and anacrusis may or

[14] An edited version may be found in Kraus, *Die Gedichte Walthers von der Vogelweide*, 45.37, 63.

60

may not be allowed; no fixed length is prescribed for stollen and *abgesang*. Yet once a definite form is chosen it is observed rigidly when, by contrast with earlier German verse, poems of more than one stanza are composed. The following stanza of this poem fits precisely the pattern of the first. It was one of the weaknesses of this period of precise form that the rhythmic restrictions did not permit variation in rhythm to accompany variation in sense, such as Heine used with effect in *Die zwei Grenadiere;* the basic rhythm may be illustrated by the first line:

Nach Frankreich zogen zwei Grenadier
    With France as goal marched two grenadiers

but the rhythm shifts to anapests when the grenadier thinks of the riding emperor:

Dann reitet mein Kaiser wohl über mein Grab
    My emperor will gallop then over my grave

The hapless successors of the minnesinger exploited this formal weakness in full. But in the period of classical Middle High German verse the balance between strictness and freedom encouraged a high standard of poetry.

Another of the required restrictions for Middle High German lyric poets was the need of developing new forms for new poems. To be sure they usually adhered to a tripartite division in their lyrics, but varied the segments of their form —the number of lines per stanza, the number of stresses, the use of anacrusis, the type of rime, and so on. The Middle High German epic poets in general maintain the rimed couplets, but even in his epic poem *Titurel,* Wolfram experimented with a stanzaic form. In this period of extension in Germany the characteristic elements of the new form were under complete control, were greatly developed in their possibilities, and were combined with their subject matter so that one could

61

with difficulty see further possibilities of development of this particular form. For centuries after this time poets were busy applying the innovations of the thirteenth-century authors.

In England, alliterative poetry did not yield to end-rime verse until the techniques of the Latin poetry had been perfected, until its rhythms were relatively smooth, and its rimes pure. For Latin poetry, after providing the initial pattern for Celtic and Germanic end-rime verse, seems to have been influenced by these. By the twelfth century the rimes in the Latin poems extended to the stem syllables. Whether English poetry in end rime was based on these, or on French poetry, the earliest that we have after the Norman conquest lacks the crudities of Otfrid, although for mastery of form equaling that of the twelfth-century Middle High German poets we must wait until the time of Chaucer. To be sure, Layamon's *Brut* shows a confusion of the old and new rhythms, comparable to Otfrid's *Krist*. But its contemporary, *The Owl and the Nightingale,* has few difficulties with the four-stress couplet or with its rimes. Many of the problems that Otfrid faced had probably been solved in the English poetry that has not come down to us, and others had been surmounted in the patterns for Middle English verse. In the poems between Layamon and Chaucer skill in the form was increased; the rhythm of the *Genesis* of 1250 is as smooth as that of contemporary lyrics. By the time Chaucer began writing, the new form was under complete control and ready for a master-poet. Chaucer made use of its formal possibilities, restoring English poetry to a height unknown since the *Beowulf*.

Accordingly, by the thirteenth century the various Germanic languages had turned from the original Germanic verse form to the Latin-Romance form. Though the rate and course of change varies, in none of the three important literary areas of the Germanic world was verse form still governed by the Germanic principles. In Iceland, the most conservative area, alliteration was still retained as a structural feature, but in combination with rime and regular rhythm; in the main stream of poetry of the English area, and in the German area, alliteration had merely become a stylistic feature. Apart from Icelandic verse—which never again reached its early dominant position in Germanic literature—and the alliterative poetry of north England, the Germanic world had turned completely from irregular rhythm and alliteration to even rhythm and rime.

3 CHANGE IN FORM AND LINGUISTIC STRUCTURE

Poetic and Linguistic Rhythm

Just as the various Germanic peoples once shared a common language, so they used the same verse form. But, as was demonstrated in the preceding chapter, the earliest records that have come down to us from areas with noteworthy literary achievement show variety in both linguistic and poetic form. In dealing with the developments from Proto-Germanic to the various languages we shall concern ourselves only with the four older Germanic languages that need be taken into account for the purpose of most literary investigations: Old English, the language of England; Old Saxon, the language of northern Germany; Old High German, the language of southern Germany; Old Norse, the language of Norway, especially in the slight variant of this used in Iceland, which is more accurately called Old Icelandic. In both forms, linguistic and poetic, the differences between these areas became progressively greater.

Old English and Old Norse of the ninth century were probably mutually intelligible; Old English and Old Saxon surely were, though it is questionable whether Old Norse would have been understood by a North German, and especially by a South German, or their languages by an Old Norse speaker. The alliterative line in the three areas differs too, with England again occupying a middle position.

By the thirteenth century the language differences would probably not have permitted mutual comprehension among any of these languages. And the verse structures were quite disparate: the north had developed the alliterative line to a tightly packed unit; Germany had given it up; and English poets were choosing between the alliterative and the rimed forms.

In investigating the changes in Germanic poetic form, it would be difficult to deny a relation between them and the linguistic changes. Germanic verse form was constructed out of the patterns of colloquial speech, out of the rhythms of prose. Changes in these would effect changes in poetic form wherever this continued to be based on the prose rhythms. Yet what specific relationships can we find between changes in linguistic and poetic form? Can changes in rhythm be correlated with any particular linguistic changes such as changes in accent, in the frequency of long or short syllables, in grammar, e.g., the introduction of compound tenses, or with changes in vocabulary? Do parallel linguistic developments lead to parallel poetic changes, or can poetic developments be found which do not accord with the changes in language?

There is little doubt about the parallelism between the employment of actual speech rhythms and the success of a poetic form. The Alexandrine has never yielded high poetry in English or German, though it is the common verse pattern in French. Its success depends on a smooth accent structure with delicate nuances; the line becomes absurd in the relatively vigorous, alternating stress patterns of English and German. Conversely the use of blank verse is impossible in French. Likewise, attempts to introduce into English and German classical meters based on variations in syllabic quantity have failed; again the linguistic basis of the classical rhythm, syllabic quantity, is nonsignificant in these languages.

65

The requirements for a successful poetic form were no different in the earlier Germanic languages; when, as in late Skaldic verse, speech rhythms and poetic form became incompatible, the form degenerated to a game and had to be sustained by artificial devices.

Relations between change in language and change in poetic structure have been recognized, but the discussion of them is usually confined to external, almost superficial, elements of the language, such as changes in vocabulary. After dealing with the variety of rhythms in Layamon, Saintsbury asks: "Does not this immense mass of apparently confused experiment suggest that the language itself has passed into a new rhythmical atmosphere? that two different metrical systems . . . were sounding in Layamon's brain?"[1] Saintsbury, unfortunately, confuses rhythmical systems found in the language with the metrical systems derived from them by poets. Further, he restricts the causes for rhythmic changes to changes in vocabulary; consequently he finds it puzzling that Layamon introduced profound changes in poetic rhythm though he employed few Romance words.

Yet poetic rhythm is much less dependent on vocabulary than on phonological features of language, such as systems of sounds, stress, pitch, and syllabic structure. The English vocabulary was considerably influenced by French in the thirteenth and fourteenth centuries, but the poetic rhythms underwent little modification during this period. Borrowed words usually are fitted into the existing rhythmic patterns. On the other hands, the rhythm of modern English poetry differs considerably from that of the nineteenth century, though in this period there have been no wholesale importations of vocabulary into English. If we wish to understand the rhythms of any language, we must proceed beyond the

[1] George Saintsbury, *A History of English Prosody* (London, The Macmillan Company, 1906), 139.

66

externals and analyze its system of sounds and note their frequency. For sounds or combinations of sounds may occur in two different languages but differ entirely in their effect. English, in words like *penknife* and *cattail,* possesses the double consonants that help to make Italian so mellifluous as a poetic language, but inasmuch as these words are relatively rare, at least in a poetic vocabulary, an English poet could not hope to achieve with them the effect of Italian long consonants.

Later in his discussion of the changes in Layamon, Saintsbury again fails to distinguish between the rhythms of speech and those that a poet chooses to employ. For he goes on to say that if a student is acquainted with Old English, Middle English, and Modern English poetry he will perceive that in Layamon there is

something much more than a mere regularizing of accentual verse with the addition of rhyme, something much more than a mere imitation of French and Latin models. . . . The prosody of English was changing from accent and alliteration to feet and rhyme; but it was not following French, or the general run of medieval Latin, in adopting syllabic uniformity as a rule; and it was, in a large number, if not the majority of instances, allowing the substitution of equivalent feet (especially anapaests for iambs) exactly as some, but not all, classical metre had allowed it.[2]

Here, too, Saintsbury seems to be clinging to prosodies rather than to the rhythm of English. Elsewhere he seems to hold that prosody is based on language,[3] but here it seems a thing apart, something that can adopt chosen features of the language and reject others, that can equate one rhythmic group with another. Unless we analyze a language for the elements which determine its particular rhythm, such as characterize English as opposed to French, we will have

[2] *Ibid.,* 146–47.
[3] *Ibid.,* 161.

neither a statement of its rhythm as a language, nor of the characteristic elements of its poetic rhythm.

Paradoxically enough, in a rhythmic study we cannot even deal with the sounds of a language, with physical units. While speech rhythms are carried by physical units, their appeal to the speakers is not through such units but rather through classes abstracted from these. Though not meant in this way, Eliot's dictum that the "sound of a poem is as much an abstraction as is the sense"[4] becomes even more significant when examined with the principles of modern linguistics. For it is now demonstrated that speakers of a language deal not with sounds but with abstractions, usually referred to as phonemes. A naïve speaker of Italian does not recognize a difference between the final sounds of English *sin* and *sing,* for in his language these belong to one abstracted class, to one phoneme; the speakers of English, however, who have learned to sort out the phonemes in their language, consider such sounds quite distinct. On the other hand, they fail to recognize a difference between the initial sounds of *coon* and *keen* that speakers brought up on some other linguistic system, such as Eskimo, would have no trouble distinguishing.

Employment of abstractions rather than sounds is also in evidence when words are imported into a language, or a new language acquired. In learning German, speakers of English generally substitute their own diphthongs for German long vowels, because they have abstracted oppositions between diphthongs and somewhat shorter vowels, e.g., *meet* and *mitt* where German has oppositions between long and short vowels, as in *mied* 'avoided' and *mit* 'with'. The reliance of language on abstractions rather than on sounds has been further demonstrated by physical measurements of sounds in the same language; the same physical sound made by two different speakers may correspond to two different

[4] Eliot, *The Music of Poetry,* 19.

phonemes. Conversely, the same phoneme of different speakers, as the vowel of *set,* may be made up of demonstrably different physical events.[5] We could scarcely find better proof that the understanding of a language and interpretation of speech is effected through the recognition of abstract entities, not through that of physical elements. It is with such abstractions that current linguistics deals, in contrast with the physical entities of nineteenth-century linguistics; and with such we must deal in the analysis of poetic rhythm.

Similar abstractions must be determined for the other elements that make up rhythm—duration, stress, and syllabic structure. Here too physical entities fail to correspond to linguistic categories. The vowel *æ,* as in English *cat,* is by measurement one of the longest vocalic sounds, yet it patterns with the short vowels; like the vowels of *kit* and *cut* it never stands finally in a word. Probably because of this patterning it is quite falsely labeled by many speakers and handbooks of English as a "short vowel." Here again the speakers of a language ignore physical differences in favor of linguistic patterns.

For the several abstractions—significant sound-classes or phonemes, significant duration, stress, syllabic structure— a system exists in every language. Learning these systems is one of the processes involved in learning the language. And on them the language rhythms are built. These systems the poet can ignore no more than the less gifted speaker. If a poet attempted to revise the system—if he, for example, should wish to introduce double consonants like those of Italian into English poetry, his audience would completely disregard his innovations or find them queer distortions that they themselves would ignore if they should choose to read such poetry. A poet is therefore limited by his linguistic material; even noteworthy deviations from prose vocabulary, e.g., the clas-

[5] See Martin Joos, *Acoustic Phonetics* (Baltimore, 1948), 55 ff.

sical names found in Milton or the foreign words used by modern poets such as Pound and Eliot, can effect only minor changes in speech rhythms which might occur from distortions in the frequency of certain sounds that foreign words may bring about in an English text. The sounds in these borrowings which differ from English sounds cannot have any effect on the rhythm because the hearer ignores them, substituting those that are most similar in his own language. If then we determine the rhythmic systems in any given language we know the limitations of poetic rhythms in that language.

Just as the physical entities of speech may serve different functions in various languages, e.g., the final sound of *sing* in English and Italian, so may structural patterns. In Old Icelandic verse, e.g., the first syllable of *búa* is usually classed as short together with the first syllable of *geta;* in Old English verse, patterns like *bú(a)* are classed as long, but patterns like *ge(ta)* as short. In different languages, and in different periods of one language, the same structural pattern may vary in its effect. Consequently, a direct comparison of the sounds of two different languages outside of their systems would be worthless. The effect of any pattern can be determined only from the structure in which we find it; comparisons, to have any meaning, must be between systems, or parts of systems.

Moreover, prosodic patterns may differ from linguistic patterns. The Germanic alliterative sets are in general based on phonemic sets. In the Germanic languages |p| and |b| are different phonemes, and each alliterates only with itself. But in two respects the Germanic alliterative sets differ from the phonemic sets: (1) *sp, st, sk* are not distinct phonemes, yet *sp* alliterates only with *sp, st* with *st, sk* with *sk;* and (2) the various vowels and diphthongs alliterate interchangeably, *a* with itself, or with *e,* or *i,* etc. In Germanic alliterative poetry, the prosodic set of consonants is larger than is the phonemic set, that of vowels much smaller. In Germanic rimed verse too the prosodic possibilities correlate rather closely with phonemic sets, though not completely, as in modern English where rimes like *winter-wind* : *kind* are permitted. When poetic and linguistic patterns do not coincide, it is true in the Germanic languages, and apparently in other languages too, that the prosodic systems are the smaller. Prosodic systems seem not to make full use of the possibilities latent in a linguistic system. If a poetic school neglects too many linguistic possibilities, however, it will generally not be esteemed highly, and will probably be superseded by an innovating group as the German poets of the tenth and eleventh centuries with their weak stock of rimes were succeeded by Wolfram and Walther. Similarly a poet who fails to exploit his linguistic possibilities, such as one who constantly constructs his rimes of the same material, is monotonous and dull.

While then every language has a definable system of sound-classes, this system may or may not be fully utilized in its poetry. But to determine the possible poetic system, we must first analyze the linguistic system. It may be worth noting here too that languages fail to exploit the possible linguistic material. As a simple example from two Indo-European languages, modern English has a stock of final clusters, as in *winds, shifts, texts,* that Russian finds impossible, only in turn to have initial clusters, as in |fpskof| 'to Pskov', that perplex a speaker of English. There is no inherent reason why English should permit clusters of four consonants finally and not initially; or Russian the converse. That they do not, however, limits the possible words, the sound system, and the poetic system of both languages. Without such linguistic information, and it is rare in works dealing with prosody, we cannot give an accurate picture of poetic rhythm.

The Elements of Germanic Rhythm

Theoretically the rhythm of a language may be composed of many elements: variation in stress, in pitch, in syllabic structure, and in phonetic characteristics. Of these, modern English utilizes chiefly stress. Variations in syllabic pitch, between syllables with a high tone and a low tone such as existed in ancient Greek and Sanskrit, are not significant in English words. Likewise, variation in syllabic structure is nonsignificant; *parched,* for example, does not fall into a syllabic group different from syllables like *par,* or *pa,* though actually it is considerably longer.

Nor in verse do we demand that syllables important to the rhythm have a characteristic pitch, that they be long or short, or that they end in a particular consonant or group of consonants. Stress makes up the backbone of modern English poetic rhythm. Color is added by means of variation in sentence pitch and in syllabic structure, and especially in sound. Most obvious of the nonessential components are end rimes. More subtle devices are also used—internal rimes, dwelling on a particular sound, relation of sound patterns to meaning —and it was these that Stevenson admired in the following passage from *Antony and Cleopatra* (II.2.206)[6] (the italics are his):

The *b*arge she sat *in,* like a *burn*ish'd throne
Burn'd *on* the water: the *poop* was *b*eaten gold;

[6] R. L. Stevenson, "On Some Technical Elements of Style in Literature," Essays in the Art of Writing, *The Biographical Edition of the Works* (New York, 1923), 253-77, especially 273.

*Pur*ple the sails, and so *per*fumed that
The winds were love-sick with them;

The essential rhythmic component here is the stress, and its distribution. Yet as Stevenson noted, and as any reader can establish by recalling other passages from Shakespeare, the bilabial stops *p* and *b* here occur with such frequency and so interlaced with *r* and *n* patterns that their presence must have been intended. The elements that appealed to Stevenson are in no way essential to the rhythm of English blank verse; they belong rather to the lowest levels of the meaning. Shakespeare's manipulation of the labials *p* and *b,* of the *ur* sequence, and of *n,* produces no constant semantic reaction in his audience, but rather an indefinable effect like that of music, pleasing yet varying from person to person.

Other verse is similarly composed of elements which are required by the prevailing poetic form, and of elements which are ancillary to it and ornamental. For example, alliteration was a required element of early Germanic verse; rime, however, ornamental. In medieval Germanic verse these roles were reversed, with rime now essential. In modern English and German verse neither is essential. Studies of poetic form must distinguish carefully between essential and ancillary rhythmic elements, or they will be reduced to statements of personal opinion.

Inasmuch as the poetic rhythm of modern English relies primarily on one linguistic characteristic, it is relatively simple. We cannot assume that the rhythm of English poetry always has been so, even though stress has always been an essential element of English and Germanic poetic rhythm. For components which make up the rhythm of a language not only may be utilized or disregarded but may also be utilized in various degrees. Though two languages may make use of stress accent in marking their rhythm, the stress may be used in each to completely different effect. The stress of French is

73

much less emphatic than is that of modern English; and the stress of modern English may well be less than was that of older English, or that of the other early Germanic languages.

In modern English poetry it is sentence stress rather than word or syllable stress that makes up the rhythm. Words from any part of speech may occupy a position of stress, as may be illustrated from the *Antony and Cleopatra* passage cited above: nouns, e.g., *barge;* verbs, e.g., *burn'd;* adjectives, e.g., *purple;* adverbs, e.g., *so;* conjunctions, e.g., *that,* etc. Furthermore, a word may occupy an accented position in one line, an unaccented a few lines later. In the oldest Germanic poetry syllable or word stress determined the occurrence of a word in the lift or drop. Nouns characteristically occupied the lifts. Any noun which was used in the lifts was generally avoided in the drops. In the *Beowulf,* for example, *god* 'God' occurs thirty-two times, occupying one of the three first lifts in all occurrences but four; furthermore, in twenty-two of these occurrences it alliterates, occupying the important third lift in twenty-one instances. Only four of the twenty-four occurrences of the finite forms of *standan,* however, occupy one of the three first lifts of the line; only one of these the third position. Nouns occupy most of the first three lifts in the older Germanic poetry because their word stress was much stronger than was that of verbs, and because in this poetry word stress was relatively much more important than was sentence stress.

Differences of pitch were, as far as we know, of no significance in molding the form of Germanic poetry. We are sure that the pitch was not used to distinguish words, as it is in Chinese (where pitch alone distinguishes *măi* 'buy' from *mài* 'sell'), or Japanese, where pitch, not stress, variation makes up the accentual pattern of words. But in phrases and sentences the older Germanic languages probably made use of pitch, much as does modern English or German. Morgan even attempted to explain the preference for certain words in the alliterative scheme by assuming that they agreed in pitch pattern.[7] He scarcely proceeded beyond this assumption, formulating no scheme for the Germanic pitch patterns which could then be applied to support his thesis. Since most of the alliterations are based on stress it is difficult to find lines to test Morgan's assumption. Some lines fail to fit it; in *Heliand* 1545*b*, for example, *mannun* occupies a poetic stress in the phrase *gôdun mannun*, but not in the same phrase in line 1766*a* where the intonation pattern must have been the same. Unless further study can find recurrent pitch patterns, we can as well justify the variation in choice of particular alliterating words by taste of the author, or by meaning patterns. Like variations in sound in modern English poetry, variations in pitch may have lent color to the Germanic line without contributing to its essential rhythm.

Syllabic structure, though, was vitally important; with stress it made up the essential rhythmic pattern. Unlike modern English, Germanic syllables had to fit certain requirements for quantity as well as for stress before occupying the predominant locations in the rhythm: these requirements led to the terms *lift* (German *Hebung*) and *drop* (German *Senkung*) rather than the terms *accented* and *unaccented syllables* which are employed for the rhythmically predominant and subordinate syllables of modern poetry. Syllables in the lift were in general required to bę longer than syllables in the drop. In *Beowulf* 320

Strǣt wæs stānfāh,   stīg wīsode

the second syllable, *wæs,* is shorter than is the first; in the second foot, *stānfāh,* however, the quantities are equal, and only the stress makes *stān-* predominant in the compound.

---

[7] B. Q. Morgan, "Zur Lehre von der Alliteration in der westgermanischen Dichtung," *PBB,* 33 (1908), 95-181; see also Claude M. Lotspeich, "Musical Accent and Double Alliteration in the Edda," *Modern Philology,* 6 (1909), 375-84.

Likewise *wæs* is equal to *wī-* in quantity, but not in stress. In all Germanic languages short syllables usually occupied the drops, and, except under defined conditions such as resolution, long syllables the lifts. Quantity was not determined solely by counting a number of quantitative elements; in all Germanic verse a lift could be occupied as well by a short stressed syllable followed by another short as by a stressed long. On the other hand, a drop could be occupied by a long syllable. As a result metrical requirements were satisfied by many different quantitative patterns.

Since there was no metrical bar against quantitatively long syllables in the drops and short syllables in the lifts, the sound systems of the various Germanic dialects might yield totally different rhythms although the same prosodic patterns were maintained. Some dialects showed complete parallelism of contrast between short and long vowels, such as Old Norse with *i* and *í, e* and *é, a* and *á, o* and *ó, u* and *ú.* In Old English too there was relatively complete parallelism, unlike modern English where all feeling for a contrast between short and long vowels has been lost, as one may note from the use of the term "short vowel" for one of the longest sounds, the vowel of *sad.* Moreover, in the older Germanic languages there was a contrast between short and long consonants; in Old Norse, such a contrast was lacking for only two phonemes, *þ* and *h.* Accordingly, there existed a great variety in quantity of syllables: those ending in short vowels; short vowels followed by one or two consonants, occasionally more; long vowels; and long vowels followed by one or two consonants, rarely more.

The basic rhythm of any of the Germanic languages depended on the frequency of these syllabic types and on the weight of the stresses. In Old Norse, syllables ending in short vowels were relatively infrequent; in Old Saxon, relatively frequent. Consequently, these two languages would make completely different forms of theoretically the same metrical pattern. What the language patterns were we know from linguistic investigations. It remains to review these, and to illustrate their effect on the development of poetic form.

The Rhythm of Proto-Germanic

Our knowledge of Proto-Germanic, the language from which developed the various Germanic dialects, is based on conclusions drawn from historical linguistics, for, unfortunately, we have no certain records of the language itself, apart from names transmitted by classical authors, e.g., *Marcomanni,* or borrowings, which as in Finnish *kuningas* preserve an older form of the language. The oldest runic inscriptions, however, though found in North Germanic territory, closely resemble reconstructed Proto-Germanic, and may even date from the time when South Germanic peoples lived next to the North Germanic peoples whose descendants remained in the areas where the oldest runes are found; they may therefore be interpreted as Proto-Germanic material, especially since the authors seem to have maintained an archaic language for their runic inscriptions. Many of the inscriptions alliterate, and some of them fit the pattern of the Germanic poetic line.

The Gallehus horn inscription is one of these; it consists of thirty-two runes (four times the magic number eight), making up one alliterative line:

Ek HlewagastiR HoltijaR   horna tawidō.

Ek stood in anacrusis, the initial syllables of the three following substantives had primary stresses and alliterated; the final verb merely had secondary stress and it lacked alliteration. As was pointed out above, rhythmically the line fulfills the needed requirements.

A somewhat later inscription, that on the Tune stone, may even give us an early form of the northern half-stanza of *ljóðaháttr,* although we cannot be certain whether the author intended this, for we know the italicized portions of the inscription only by conjecture. If designed as verse, this inscription contains the same loose rhythmic pattern as does that on the Gallehus horn:

Ek WīwaR after Wōdurīdē   wita*n*dahalaiban worahtō *rūnōR;*
*þē*R Wōdurīdē staina   prijōR dohtriR dālidun,
     arbija arjōstēR arbijanō.
I, Wiwar, hereon for Wodurid,   the warder of bread,
                worked the runes;
   for thee, Wodurid, the stone   three daughters prepared,
     and the funeral feast the first of the heirs.

Some of the elements of Proto-Germanic rhythm, that is, the syllabic structure, we can determine from these inscriptions; for the stresses we must rely on linguistic evidence.

From the point of view of syllabic structure the Germanic line is remarkably light. Six of the thirteen syllables of the Gallehus inscription are short, seven long; of these only one contains a long vowel, and this falls in an inflectional ending. The rhythm of the Tune inscription is somewhat heavier: thirteen of the syllables are short, twelve contain short vowels followed by a consonant, thirteen a long vowel, five a long vowel followed by a consonant. Nonetheless, the line contrasts markedly in quantity with those in the later North Germanic languages.

The stress accent of these lines and of Proto-Germanic, however, must have been quite heavy. For in our earliest dialect records, final vowels which Proto-Germanic had maintained from Proto-Indo-European are lost;[8] *horna* of the

        [8] A high proportion of short syllables was maintained in Proto-

Gallehus inscription later shows up everywhere as a monosyllable. Likewise the *i* of *-gastiR* has disappeared, so that the cognate is *gastR* in Old Norse, and with further loss *giest* in Old English, *gast* in Old High German and Old Saxon. Moreover, weakly stressed medial vowels disappeared. Such wholesale losses we can ascribe only to a strong initial stress accent.

From the combination of these two characteristics—a high proportion of short syllables and a strong stress accent—we can assume a violent rhythm for Proto-Germanic verse. Proto-Germanic syllabic articulation would have increased the staccato effect of the rhythm. For from the consonant changes we can infer that the juncture between syllables was similar to that between words, inasmuch as the Germanic consonants underwent the same shift, unlike the later Old High German consonants, whether they stood medially or initially in words. Proto-Indo-European *d* became Proto-Germanic *t,* for example, both initially, as in the word for *two,* compare Latin *duo,* and medially, as in the word for *eat,* compare Latin *edere.* Only when a consonant preceded in the syllable did the sound remain unshifted, as in *-gastiR,* compare Latin *hostis. Hle-wa-ga-stiR* then was pronounced with four neatly distinguished syllables.

The rhythmic irregularity of the Germanic line would have been even more marked because of the variation in length of the rhythmical units. Since the first syllable of every word was strongly stressed, each word or element of a compound formed one rhythmical unit, yielding prosodic units varying like those of the Gallehus inscription between four, three, and two syllables. For the result one could hardly find a more fitting adjective than Tacitus' *inconditus.* Yet Tacitus was no more perplexed by the rhythm than were nineteenth-century scholars. Only extensive compilations of Sievers and his

Germanic because the change from a pitch to a stress accent occurred relatively late in the Proto-Germanic period.

school revealed a small number of similar underlying rhythmical patterns; these, later metrists, especially Heusler, have restated in terms of time units.

Between Proto-Germanic and the period of the dialects the languages underwent tremendous changes which were by no means parallel. The strong initial stress accent continued to contribute to a shortening of words and a modification of syllabic structure. In those dialects in which the primary stress remained strong the proportion of heavy syllables increased greatly. In those dialects in which it was reduced in intensity the short syllables are much more prominent. Our earliest verse in the various dialects therefore produces strikingly different effects, and effects unlike those of Proto-Germanic verse.

The Rhythm of Old Norse

The North Germanic dialects were those in which the Germanic syllabic structure was most drastically modified. After the sound changes which took place between Proto-Germanic and Old Norse the language contained a much greater proportion of long syllables than had Proto-Germanic, or than did any of the other Germanic dialects. The northern poetry too contains a preponderance of them, to the point of turgidity.

That the poets had no other choice may be illustrated from the preponderance of long syllables in prose. In a random passage of Old Norse prose written at the beginning of the thirteenth century, a selection from the *Landnamabók,* only one out of every four syllables is short; in a passage written around 1300, from the *Njáls saga,* the proportion is just a bit higher. The following table gives the number of

80

syllables of various structure, with those of the Tune and Gallehus inscriptions added for comparison:

	Land.	Njáls	Tune	Gall.
⌣	37	46	13	6
⌣C	82	61	12	6
⌣CC	25	27	..	.
—	18	19	13	1
—C	23	13	5	.
—CC	4	2	..	.

In comparison with the runic passages the frequency of long syllables is very high. And the alliterative line of the *Edda* contrasts markedly with that on the Gallehus horn. The first stanza of the *Song of Weland* contains only four prosodically short syllables, all but one in inflectional endings; these are italicized:

Meyiar fl*ugo* sunnan,
  Myrkvið í gǫgnom,
alvitr ungar,
  ørlǫg drýgi*a*.
Þær á sævar strǫnd
  settoz at hvílaz,
drósir suðrœnar,
  dýrt lín spunn*o*.

       Maidens flew from the south
          through Myrkvið,
       winsome Valkyries,
          warfare to arouse.
       There on the sea shore
          they sat to rest,
       daughters of the south,
          dear linen span.

The preponderance of long syllables is not difficult to explain when one examines the sound changes of Proto-North Germanic. Nearly all of them are directed towards an increase in quantity. Many final syllables were lost; the nominative, genitive, and accusative singular inflections of "fish" in Proto-North Germanic comprised two syllables each, in Old Norse all of them are monosyllables which are prosodically long:

PNGmc.	nom.	fiskaR	ON	fiskr
	gen.	fiskas		fisks
	acc.	fiska		fisk

A similar loss in verbal forms may be illustrated by the second singular present, which again became monosyllabic in most verbs, e.g.,

PNGmc. bindiR 'you tie'   ON bindr.

Other sound changes contributed to the number of lengthened consonants without reducing the quantity of preceding vowels. In this way medial vowels were syncopated in some weak verbs; compare Gothic *fōdida* and Old Norse *fødda* 'nourished'. After such vowel losses, one of the contiguous consonants was often assimilated to the other, as in PNGmc. *hailaR*, Old Norse *heill* 'hail'. Furthermore, there were contractions, as in PNGmc. *haðuk-*, Old Norse *hauk-* 'hawk'; the cognate of Gothic *frijōnds* in Old Norse, *frǽndr* 'relative', is monosyllabic and heavy. Some short final vowels were lengthened even when no consonants were lost, as in *sá* 'he', *suá* 'so', etc. Even though long vowels were shortened sporadically, introducing short syllables, the great majority of sound changes produced the opposite effect.

From a language with a reasonable balance between short and long syllables there had developed one with a great preponderance of longs. Nor do we find in Old Norse the high proportion of polysyllabic words with short medial and final syllables that is in evidence in the runic inscriptions. A glance at any Old Norse prose text will disclose few polysyllables; most of these are personal or place names.

Even the morphological changes failed to introduce light, weakly stressed syllables. On the one hand, North Germanic did not develop as many weakly stressed verbal and nominal modifiers as did the West Germanic languages. In the north the present and preterite forms maintained their uses more completely than did their cognates in the south. Articles and verbal auxiliaries make up a great part of the word-indices of Middle High German poets; when one compares an index of Old Norse material one finds a much lower proportion of them. Even such new forms as were developed in Old Norse increased rather than decreased the number of heavy syllables. A passive was made by suffixing *sk* to existing verb forms; this contributed further heavy syllables, whereas its equivalent in the south introduced weakly stressed auxiliaries. Likewise the northern postpositive article contributed weight in contrast to the articles of the south. And prefixes, such as the relatively common *gi-* in the preterite participle, were not used commonly in the north. Consequently North Germanic morphological developments occasion nothing like the great number of light, weakly stressed syllables which arise in the West Germanic languages.

Fortunately, an excellent grammatical treatise from about 1150 gives us a description of contemporary Old Icelandic. The vowel system at the time was composed of nine members, all of which existed in long as well as short form, as well as nasalized (i.e., prosodically long); six diphthongs contributed further to the preponderance of long vowels. Moreover, all but one of the thirteen postvocalic consonants could be long as well as short, and long consonants could stand after long vowels as well as after short. The grammar confirms our views on the heaviness of the language.[9]

Yet in spite of the tendency to monosyllabism the primary stress was strong. This is clear from the continued loss of weakly stressed syllables. While Proto-Germanic was characterized by a heavy stress on the first syllable of words which

[9] It is most conveniently available in the edition and translation of Einar Haugen, *First Grammatical Treatise* (Baltimore, 1950).

could vary greatly in length, Old Norse maintained the heavy stress, though in short words composed of heavy syllables. Small wonder that the requirements of the alliterative half-line were often satisfied with four syllables. Even in the old *Song of Weland* the half-lines rarely contain as many as six syllables, never as many as the Gallehus inscription, and may even contain less than four, as in stanza 11, line 2*b*:

Sat hann svá lengi,
  at hann sofnaði;
ok hann vaknaði
  vilia lauss:
vissi sér á hǫndom
  hǫfgar nauðir,
en á fótom
  fiǫtur um spentan.
    Sat then so long
      that he slumbered,
    but he wakened
      wanting joy:
    felt on his hands
      heavy bonds,
    and on his feet
      fastening chains.

The tendency to restrict the number of syllables in Eddic poetry grew rather than lessened, and in the *Hávamál* some of the most famous half-lines are made up of but two syllables, only the lifts: *deyr fé*.

Such was the popular Eddic poetry. Theoretically it maintained the freedom of Germanic verse: a variety of weakly accented syllables was permitted, effecting rhythmic patterns of different types. But the structure of the language permitted even the free Eddic verse little latitude.

Beside it there developed a much more rigid form, that of the court poets or skalds. The skalds added external requirements to those they had inherited: (1) internal rime of various types was introduced and (2) the number of syllables was fixed. In Skaldic verse, form dominated sense completely. A skald inherited his molds and had to pour his language into them. Differences from the word order of everyday speech were not rejected; an interlocking sentence pattern actually became one of the favorites, as in the last half-stanza of Sigvatr's *Bersǫglisvísur*:

Erum Mǫgnús vér vægnir,
  vildak með þér mildum
(Haralds varðar þú hjǫrvi
  haukey) lifa ok deyja.
    To your will, Magnus, yielding,
      we would with you, the good,
    (who guards with sword Harold's
      hawk-island) live and die.

Only the greatest poets wielded Skaldic form with any originality, and then with the help of artificial linguistic creations. Mythological names were very useful; since Odin was the storm-god and a sword gleamed when brandished, a sword might be called Odin's fire, or any other name of Odin's might be introduced that suited the requirements of alliteration and rhythm. Metaphors made on metaphors, the kennings, provided further phonological patterns for the required rimes; hundreds of kennings were available for common ingredients of the Skaldic occasional verse such as 'sword': simple ones like *gunneldr* 'battle-fire' based on the flashing, *blóðormr* 'blood-serpent', based on its form, *sárlax* 'wound-salmon', based on its slenderness, abstract ones like *hjalmskóð* 'helm-scathe', based on its destructiveness, and more complex ones like that for shield in the selection from Bragi cited above.

The germ of such formal devices is to be found even outside Old Norse verse. Here, however, it is ornamental, not required. In the following passage from the *Beowulf*, for example (320),

85

Strǣt wæs stānfāh,   stīg wīsode
gumun ætgædere.   Gúðbyrne scān
heard hondlocen,   hringīren scīr
song in searwum, . . .

> The road was rock-paved,   the route guided
> the warriors together.   The war-byrnies shone
> hard, arranged by hands,   ring-iron bright
> sang in the armor, . . .

the melody is not governed by the alliteration alone; lines 320 and 321*a* show a progression of repeated vowels: $\bar{æ}\ \bar{æ}$, $\bar{a}\ \bar{a}$, $\bar{\iota}\ \bar{\iota}$ (*o e*), *u u*, $\bar{æ}\ \bar{æ}$, which is taken up again in 322, *o o*, and ends in the full rime, $\bar{\iota}r$- *scīr*. The *aðalhending* of the skalds is here, though ornamental not structural, and was presumably not unknown in other old Germanic verse; it simply remained for the skalds to generalize it, to restrict its use, as they restricted the number of syllables per line. Whether this was done under the influence of Irish poetry is one of the most disputed problems in Germanic literary studies, and will be discussed below. Even though we find *aðalhendings* in the *Beowulf* we have no proof that they are Germanic in origin. For contacts with the Irish predate the writing of *Beowulf*, and may have yielded patterns for Old English as well as for Old Norse verse.

Likewise, the source of syllable-counting cannot be ascribed to any known influence. To be sure we encounter syllable-counting first in the postclassical Latin hymns of the fifth and sixth centuries; alternating lines of eight and seven syllables make up a favorite stanza. From here the practice spread to Ireland, where it replaced the older freedom in the number of stressed syllables. Most of the Irish poetry from the eighth century onward is composed of lines containing no characteristic stress patterns but only a fixed number of syllables. And with the ninth-century skalds, the principle of limiting the number of syllables is introduced into Germanic.

While the principle seems foreign in Germanic verse, the linguistic developments in the north were not unfavorable for its application. For the pattern of the Germanic alliterative half-line required two stressed syllables, each usually accompanied by a number of weakly stressed syllables. When many weakly stressed syllables were lost, when Old Norse developed towards monosyllabism, the alliterative pattern could only be maintained by awareness of the need to introduce material for the drops. One syllable was the minimum required to separate the lifts, and this minimum satisfied the northern poets. Since the line of the favorite stanza pattern of the skalds, the *dróttkvætt,* contained three stresses, it was made up of six syllables.

The earliest skalds fulfilled the requirements of syllable-counting imperfectly, as in the first line of the *stef* in Bragi's *Ragnarsdrápa*:

Ræs gǫfumk reiðar mána
Ragnarr ok fjǫlð sagna.
> Me the moon of Rae's ship gave
> Ragnar, and many a saga.
>> (Ragnar gave me a shield, with
>> many a story.)

Later the rhythm becomes almost regular, with an alternation of stressed and unstressed syllables, as in the first lines of Sturla Þórðarson's *Hrynhenda*:

Frægjan réð þik Viljálmr vígja,
varrbáls hǫtuðr, karðínáli;
> Viljalmr thee, oh famed one, hallowed,
> hater, cardinal, of gold, the sea-flood;

We find a similar development to regular rhythm in the northern prose. The Runic prose lines show marked irregularity in the number of weakly stressed syllables per stress; the late Icelandic prose can almost be scanned, e.g., *Njáls saga,* Chapter 36: *Gunn*arr *reið* til *þings,* en *áðr* hann *reið* *hei*man, *mæl*ti *hann* till *Hall*gerðar . . .; or Chapter 122:

Njáll stóð *upp* ok *mæl*ti : "*Þess* bið ek *Hall* af *Siðu* ok *Flo*sa ok *al*la *Sigfús*sonu ok *al*la *vára menn,* at þér *gangið ei*gi i *braut* ok *heyr*ið *mál* mitt." Similar and more extensive passages can be found in this and other sagas. Since the prose rhythms had become so regular, the skalds were not compelled to force their language into the new poetic rhythms ; linguistic changes almost made the new rhythm mandatory.

We see from an examination of linguistic and poetic developments that many of the characteristic poetic changes in the north correspond to changes in the language. When the majority of the weakly stressed vowels of Proto-Germanic had been lost, the northern line became very short ; rarely does more than one unaccented syllable accompany an accented. The linguistic changes, however, did not lead to abandonment of the alliterative form. For the weight of the line was maintained through a relatively strong stress accent and a preponderance of long syllables. The demands of the alliterative line were accordingly unchanged both in the later Eddic and in the Skaldic verse. The freedoms, however, were fulfilled by means of a few long syllables rather than by a number of light syllables, and as a result the line itself produced an effect completely different from that of the Proto-Germanic line.

Changes Common to the West Germanic Languages

While the North Germanic languages were becoming more and more turgid and terse, the changes in the West Germanic group produced languages almost the converse in rhythm. Both in the sound system and the form system, innovations yielded a great number of short and weakly stressed syllables. In Old High German, which carried such innovations furthest, the linguistic changes made alliterative poetry almost impossible. For syllables ending in short vowels are more frequent than any other in our Old High German prose texts; moreover, the syllables ending in long vowels or long vowels plus consonants, which in alliterative poetry counted as heavy, occur chiefly in inflectional endings. These, of course, could not occupy the lifts. In alliterative poetry constructed from such materials the linguistic structure would conflict with metrical requirements: the lifts would usually be occupied by short syllables, the drops, on the other hand, by long syllables. Since the other West Germanic languages underwent changes similar to those of Old High German, it is not strange that such alliterative poetry as we have from the West Germanic languages becomes more and more unlike the North Germanic verse.

The linguistic changes that produced these modifications in the West Germanic languages occurred gradually, and failed to cover the entire West Germanic area. Fewer of them are in evidence in the *Beowulf* than in the later Old English poems; fewer in the late Old English poems than in Old Saxon and Old High German.

Possibly the most important phonological development general to all of the West Germanic languages is a weakening of the primary stress. Our evidence for determining this leveling is taken from the treatment of vowels in syllables that did not occupy the primary stress. In Old Norse we had noted a further reduction of weakly stressed vowels beyond that of Proto-Germanic. The West Germanic languages did not reduce such vowels; the medial vowel was lost in Old Norse *batri, betri* 'better', compare Gothic *batiza,* but not in Old High German *bezziro* and Old English *betera*. Rather, the converse development was more normal; syllables in which vowels had been lost between Proto-Indo-European and

Proto-Germanic now show new vowels. In this way the cognates of Gothic *akrs,* Old Norse *akr* 'field', are *æcer* in Old English, *acer* in Old Saxon, and *accar* in Old High German; the cognates of Gothic *fugls,* Old Norse *fugl* 'bird', are *fugol* in Old English, *vogal* in Old High German, and *fugal* in Old Saxon. Such vowels develop in weakly stressed medial syllables as well as in final syllables; Old High German *gimahalta,* for example, is composed of four syllables in contrast with the two of Old Norse *mælte* 'said'. The prevalence of weakly stressed vowels in the West Germanic languages would scarcely have been possible if the strong Germanic primary stress had been maintained. From the number of weakly stressed vowels we therefore conclude that the strong initial stress was beginning to be reduced in West Germanic, a conclusion supported by uncertainty in stress patterns of West Germanic poets.

The contrast between heavy and light syllables was also removed in large measure by the West Germanic consonant lengthening. In this process, a number of consonants were lengthened before certain following consonants, especially before *j* but also before *r, l, m, n, w,* e.g., Old English *settian,* Old High German *sezzen,* but Old Norse *satja,* Gothic *satjan.* Consonants were not lengthened, however, after syllables with long vowel, as in Old English *sēcan* 'seek', Old Saxon *sōkian,* compare Gothic *ga-sōkjan.* Furthermore, consonants in clusters remained short; with Old Saxon *sendian,* compare Gothic *sandjan* 'send'. Since prosodic length was determined by short vowel and consonant as well as by long vowel, this consonant lengthening led to a regularization of stem syllables in the West Germanic languages; the syllables made heavier by the West Germanic consonant lengthening, e.g., Old Saxon *settian,* were now equal in prosodic length to those with long vowel, as Old Saxon *sōkian,* and to those with a consonant cluster, as Old Saxon *sendian.* Accordingly, after the West

Germanic consonant lengthening had been carried out we do not find the variation in syllabic quantity that had helped make Proto-Germanic and Old Norse so forceful in rhythm. Through this sound change the variation between long- and short-accented syllables was being leveled out, and with it one of the favorite rhythmic features of alliterative poetry.

While many weakly stressed syllables were introduced through phonological changes, their number does not compare with those introduced by the West Germanic morphological developments. With the other western European languages, the West Germanic languages were developing from synthetic to analytic languages. Old Norse remained far behind in this change.

Among the weakly stressed syllables were the forms of the article with the noun. Others were added in verb forms; many preterite participles came to have a *gi-* prefix; the compound tenses contributed more weakly stressed syllables in their auxiliaries. Furthermore, there was a compulsion to be explicit, to connect by means of adverbs phrases and clauses that in Old Norse would have seemed clearly related from their contiguous position. Where Old Norse reported simply and tersely Loki's flight in "feather-dress," *Þrymskviða* 5:

Fló þá Loki,
  fiaðrhamr dunði,
unz fyr útan kom
  ása garða,
ok fyr innan kom
  iǫtna heima.
> Flew then Loki
>   feather-dress resounded,
> until outside he came
>   the Aesir haunts,
> and inside he came
>   the etin's home.

Old Saxon extended the equivalent to (*Hel.* 5796) :

thuo thar suôgan quam
engil thes alouualdon   oƀana fan radure,
faran an feðerhamon,   that all thiu folda an scian,
thiu erða dunida   endi thia erlos uuurðun
an uuêkan hugie,   uuarðos Iuðeono,
bifellun bi them forahton :   ne uuândun ira fera êgan,
lîf langerun huîl.

then there approached
the angel of the Almighty   over them from the heavens
faring in feather-dress,   so that all the fields roared,
the earth resounded   and all the men became
weak in their hearts,   the wards of the Jews
fell by fear overcome :   afraid for their skins,
for longer life.

The Old Norse lines are primarily made up of content words, chiefly substantives. But the Old Saxon lines are padded with function words, *thuo, thar, that, endi,* especially articles, *thes, thiu, thiu, thia, them.* Furthermore, the Old Icelandic poet finds it unnecessary to introduce function words that relate Loki and the feather-dress; it was left to his audience to supply the relationship. The *Heliand* poet, on the other hand, is quite explicit, even using additional verbs in stating that the angel "traveled" in a feather-dress. Since the weakly stressed syllables of the increased number of function words are supplemented by those resulting from phonological changes, e.g., the extra syllables of *feðer-* and *foraht-,* the rhythm of the alliterative line is totally different.

Yet though the West Germanic languages underwent various changes that differentiated them from the northern languages, they did not remain parallel in their linguistic development; nor is their verse rhythm similar. Common to all of them is a weakening of the primary stress, as evidenced by the general development of svarabhakti vowels. Furthermore, as a result of the West Germanic consonant lengthening, many of the contrasts between light and heavy syllables came to be lost. Both linguistic developments led to greater evenness in the alliterative line, to a greater rhythmic flatness. Phonological changes affecting the rhythm and innovations in morphology varied, however, among the three West Germanic languages. Further variation is found in strength of tradition. A poetic vocabulary and conservative syntax were maintained in Old English though not in Old Saxon and Old High German. Each of the three West Germanic languages accordingly provided its poets with a different rhythm. What these were we shall note in the following sections.

The Rhythm of Old English

Of the West Germanic languages Old English was closest to Old Norse in maintaining a high preponderance of heavy stressed syllables. To this some of the linguistic innovations contributed. As in Old Norse, monosyllables ending in vowels could be lengthened, e.g., *swā* beside Gothic *swa*. This lengthening, however, was not carried through with the same thoroughness as in Old Norse; some Old English words maintained short vowels as well as long, e.g., *se* beside *sē* 'he'. Lengthening of vowels also resulted upon loss of consonants, as *sēan* beside Old Saxon *sehan* 'see', and before consonant clusters such as *ld, nd;* compare late Old English *fēld* 'field' with Old Saxon *feld,* late Old English *wōrd* 'word' with Old Saxon *uuord.* Accordingly, the proportion of heavy syllables was rather high in Old English, especially in the early period; some lines of *Beowulf* are as heavy, and short, as those of Eddic verse; for example, see *Beowulf,* lines 320 and 1324:

Yrmenlāfes   yldra brōþor,
    Yrmenlaf's   older brother,

93

Strǣt wæs stānfāh,   stīg wīsode
The road was rock-paved,   the route guided . . .

In later stages of Old English the rhythm became much lighter as further sound changes took place.

The linguistic changes which Old English underwent point to the maintenance of a relatively strong primary stress. The vowels in secondary syllables were already being weakened in the earliest stages of the language. Long vowels in syllables not containing the primary stress were shortened, in contrast with Old High German where they were maintained: compare Old High German *mahtîg* with Old English *mihtig* 'mighty', Old High German *steinîn* with Old English *stǣnen* 'of stone', Old High German *hîrât* with *hīred* 'family'. Moreover, the vowel system of weakly stressed syllables, which in West Germanic and early Old English was as complete as that in strongly stressed syllables, was being reduced; early Old English *sunu* 'son' shows up in late Old English as *sune,* early Old English *nama* 'name' as *name,* early Old English *hardost* as *hardest*. Some weakly stressed syllables were lost, as in *mǣgden* 'maiden', compare Old High German *magatîn, hwylc* 'which', compare Old High German *hwelîh*. All these weakenings indicate that the chief energy of articulation in Old English was expended on the syllables with primary stress, and that the articulation of the weakly stressed syllables was much less energetic.

While the primary stress was maintained, the secondary stresses were weakened during the Old English period. In Old High German the superlative suffix -*ôsta* kept its long vowel and its secondary stress; during Old English times both were modified as indicated by the early *hardost* but the later *hardest*. Except in compounds made up of two distinct elements, Old English words came to have one chief stress, in contrast to Proto-Germanic. In Proto-Germanic, stress was distributed according to syllables, as we may illustrate by examples from Gothic; Gothic *armōstai* 'the poorest' had a primary stress on the first syllable, a secondary stress on the second, a weak stress on the third; *aftumists* 'the last' a weak stress on the second and a secondary stress on the third. Though the first syllable of Proto-Germanic words carried the primary stress, the pattern of secondary stresses varied from word to word. And the variety in syllabic accent effected an autonomy of individual syllables. The reduction of strong secondary stresses, and the resultant development of accentual word patterns made up of a strong primary stress and one or more relatively weak, led to a shift in the articulatory units. In Proto-Germanic the articulatory and accentual unit had been the syllable; in Old English it came to be a word or a phrase. This assumption may be supported by comparison of the consonant changes occurring in Proto-Germanic and by those of the later dialects, notably Old High German. In the Proto-Germanic thoroughgoing consonant change, consonants were modified, regardless of their location in words or phrases; only their position in the syllable checked the development, as the *t* of *stand.* The shift was apparently so consistent because the articulation of consonants was not affected by their environment in words or phrases, but only by their syllabic environment. In the later Old High German shift, on the other hand, there was considerable variation of development, depending on environment in words; compare German *treu,* English *true,* where the *t* was unshifted; German *Zaun,* English *town,* where the *t* was shifted to *ts;* German *essen,* English *eat,* where the *t* was shifted to *s.* We may conclude from the diversity of developments that the articulation of consonants in Old High German, and in the other contemporary West Germanic dialects, varied considerably with the structure of words. Since sounds were differently pronounced according to their position in words, we may assume that words now formed stress units, and that metrical patterns were now

95

based on these stress units and on phrases rather than on syllables.

The greater word unity of the later dialects may also be recognized from the carry-over of articulatory patterns which characterized one portion of a word to other portions. Such carry-over effects are most notable on the vowels: the high front vowels influenced low vowels, causing the so-called *i*-umlaut; compare the Proto-Germanic *-gastiR* of the Gallehus horn with Old English *giest*. The sound *u* influenced front and low vowels; compare Old English *ealo* with Proto-Germanic *aluþ,* the vowels of which are preserved in the Lithuanian borrowing *alùs* 'beer'. Svarabhakti vowels agreed in quality with the vowels of the stressed syllables; in keeping with the back-accented vowel of *ator* 'poison' the svarabhakti vowel is back, that of *winter,* on the other hand, front. Articulatory patterns were also carried over from consonants to vowels and vice versa. Certain consonant combinations produced modifications in vowels, as Old English *neaht,* compare Gothic *nahts* 'night'. Vowels too produced modifications in consonant articulation, as Old English *ceosan* 'choose' but Old High German *kiesan*. The lack of such changes in Proto-Germanic attests a greater independence of the various sounds and syllables than was found in the later dialects; their presence in Old English suggests that words and phrases, rather than syllables, were now articulatory units.

Phenomena illustrating modifications in articulation produced by neighboring sounds are not limited to Old English; all of the Germanic dialects of which we have records after the sixth century contain examples of *i*-umlaut, most of them also of *u*-umlaut and mutual influence of consonants and vowels.

From the Proto-Germanic language which permitted great modulation of syllables, there had developed languages in which entire words and phrases were units. As a result, words and phrases, rather than syllables, came to be used to fill elements of the alliterative line, as in the following line (2357) from the *Heliand*:

Sô hêlde he thea haltun man   endi thea hâƀon sô self, . . .
    Thus he cured the lame man   and the crippled as well, . . .

The effect of the changed structure of the language is not in evidence, however, until Old Saxon and late Old English verse. *Beowulf* and the earliest Old English verse is still primarily nominal, containing a great stock of poetic compounds. Function words are kept at a minimum. Paratactic constructions are preferred in *Beowulf,* and the relation between clauses often not expressed, as in the following lines (913–15) where the antecedents of the pronouns, especially *hine,* are unclear:

               Hē þǣr eallum wearð
mǣg Higelāces   manna cynne,
frēondum gefægra ;   hine fyren onwōd.
               He [Beowulf] then to all became,
    the kinsman of Higelac,   to the folk of the court,
    to the friends a favorite ;   him [Heremod] foul sin
                          entered.

It is because of the strong poetic tradition that we find in the oldest Old English verse virtually the same stress patterns as in Old Norse Eddic verse, in spite of the linguistic changes which were taking place.

When, however, the poetic tradition begins to decline, when the stock of poetic compounds is reduced and the poetic language is based directly on that of prose, Old English verse assumes a different character. For the prose texts show a much higher percentage of short syllables than do those of Old Norse, as illustrated by the analysis of two prose passages, one from the end of the ninth century (*Al. König Alfreds d. Gr. Bearbeitung der Soliloquien des Augustus* XI. 9), another from a hundred years later (*Ael. Die Hirtenbriefe Aelfrics* IX. 6), to which the figures from one of the Old Norse passages given above are added for comparison:

	Al.	Ael.	Isl.
⌣	46	56	37
⌣C	35	71	82
⌣CC	14	3	25
—	20	16	18
—C	12	3	23
—CC	2	..	4
	129	149	189

In the Old English passages more than one of every three syllables are short; in the Old Norse, fewer than one in five. Given such material to work with the Old English poets could scarcely have maintained a rhythm similar to that of Old Norse poetry.

As a result of the increase in the number of weakly stressed syllables the weight of the alliterative line was lost, though its force was still present. The Old English poets apparently were aware of this result of the linguistic changes, and attempted to maintain the weight of the line, for they developed a means of introducing additional speech material, the so-called expanded lines. These lines contain about half again as much material as the normal lines; compare *Beowulf* 1167–68 with 1169–70:

Þæt hē hæfde mōd micel,   þēah þe hē his māgum nǽre
ārfæst æt ecga gelācum.   Sprǽc ðā ides Scyldinga:
　'Onfōh þissum fulle,   fpēodrihten mīn,
sinces brytta!'

　　　That he had great courage,   though he to his kinsmen had
　　　　　　　　　　　　　　　　　　　not been
　　　faithful in the clatter of swords.   Said then the queen of
　　　　　　　　　　　　　　　　　　　the Scyldings:

98

"Accept this chalice   dear chief mine
dispenser of treasure."

It is noteworthy that the expanded lines are poor in nominal compounds which were the elements particularly designed to convey heavy speech material in few syllables. The expanded lines of the *Beowulf* contain but two compounds, one anapestic in rhythm, the other trochaic: 1165*a suhtergefæderan* and 2996*a middangearde*. Furthermore, very few expanded lines are found in the early Old English poems, but the number of expanded lines becomes greater as the proportion of compounds decreases and that of function words increases. From one expanded line in three hundred normal lines of the *Beowulf* the proportion grows to one in six of the tenth-century *Judith;* and in an equal number of lines the *Judith* contains three times as many forms of the article as does the *Beowulf*. By the tenth century the Old English rhythm was apparently so light that the normal lines seemed to contain too few syllables.

Linguistic changes in the tenth and eleventh centuries contributed further to a decrease in weight. Vowels were shortened in various phonetic patterns, as in trisyllables, e.g., *mōnandæg* to *Monendai* 'Monday', before consonant clusters, e.g., *fiftig* 'fifty' as compared with *fīf* 'five', and even occasionally before simple consonants, e.g., *fōt* to *fott* 'foot'. The shortening of vowels before consonant clusters is of special importance in the development of rhythm, for it deprived compounds of much of their weight, e.g., *wīsdōm* to *wisdom,* and thereby removed one of the mainstays of the alliterative rhythm. Moreover, as certain words came to be used more commonly as function words, they were shortened; an example is *ān* 'one', which was the origin of the indefinite article 'an, a' as well as of the numeral 'one'. In the *Beowulf* and Cynewulf poems *ān* was treated like other cardinal numerals; when standing before a noun it alliterated. In the *Judith* it may not alliterate, as in line 325, or it may, as in lines 64 and 95; in line 325 *ān* was weakly stressed because it had already developed to an indefinite article.

As a result of the linguistic changes both word and phrasal patterns contributed to a rhythm consisting of an alternation of stressed and weakly stressed syllables, with quantity almost completely disregarded. Shortening of vowels in compounds yielded patterns like *wifman, wimman* 'women' from *wīf* plus man, *huswif* 'housewife' from *hūs* plus *wīf*. Phrasal patterns led to *aweg* from *onweg* from *on weg*, to *-del* from *-dǣl*—in patterns like *any del*. Such an alternating rhythm already pervades some of the expanded lines of the *Judith,* for example 91–94:

þearlmōd þeoden gumena: nāhte ic þīnre næfre
miltse þon māran þearfe.   Gewrec nū, mihtig dryhten,
torhtmōd tīres brytta,   þæt mē ys þus torne on mōde,
hāte on hreðre mīnum.

      stern emperor of men: never had I of thy
      mercy the more need.   Avenge now mighty Lord,
      noble Author of glory,   that there is anger in my mind,
      hate in this soul of mine.

While alternating rhythm is by no means carried through in this passage, compare 93*b;* lines 91, 93*a,* and 94*a* fall into a trochaic pattern, 92*b* into an iambic.

With the further weakening of inflectional endings after the time of composition of the late Old English poems such as the *Judith,* the alternating rhythm is almost mandatory. The Middle English rimed poetry readily observes it; even the alliterative writings cannot avoid it. For the sake of maintaining the alliterative rhythm the *Judith* poet had modified the natural accentual patterns; in line 40 the dative of *Judith* bears two chief accents, whereas elsewhere the name, though in the nominative, bears one. The fourteenth-century *Gawain* poet, on the other hand, modified alliterative technique in accordance with the new rhythm, introducing three alliterations in 17 per cent of his first half-lines, for example, lines 920, 2061, 2492, 1990:

God hatȝ geuen vus his grace   godly for soþe,
   God has given us his grace   godly forsooth,

His schalk schewed hym his schelde,   on schulder he hit laȝt,
   His servant showed him his shield,   on his shoulder he it
                                           lays,

Þe kyng kysseȝ þe knyȝt,   and þe whene alce,
   The king kisses the knight,   and the queen also,

And blyþely broȝt to his bedde   to be at his rest. . . .
   And gladly brought to his bed   to be at rest. . . .

The rhythm of such lines can hardly be distinguished from that of contemporary rimed poetry. By the time of writing of the *Gawain* poem and the other Middle English alliterative poetry, the alliterative verse differs from rimed verse only externally; the rhythm of both types is alike, but different syllables or parts of syllables in the line agree in sound.

The way for the complete adoption of the new rimed forms had long ago been provided. As poets turned from alliteration to rime, more and more relatively unstressed syllables came to stand in alliteration, such as the copula in *Judith* 255:

in ðām wlitegan træfe   wæron ætsomne
   in the wondrous tent   were together

or that in line 1990 of the *Gawain* poem cited above. Apparently the alliteration of such weakly stressed syllables, though externally filling the demands of the alliterative poetry, no longer was adequate to hold the line together. Since the initial syllables stood out so little, the Latin device of end rime was a much more effective binding force.

Judith already contains 114 rimes, 24 of which extend to the stem syllable, as in lines 2 and 23,

in ðȳs ginnan grunde;   hēo ðār ðā gearwe funde
  in this gaping ground;   she there girded found
hlōh ond hlȳdde,   hlynede ond dynede,
  laughed and brawled   roared and dinned

The *Judith* rimes have a stylistic rather than a structural function. They do not replace alliteration but are introduced when the author wishes to call attention to sounds, as in line 23 above, and in line 110:

þone hǣðenan hund,   þæt him þæt hēafod wand
  that heathen hound,   so that his head would bound

or they indicate the beginning or the close of an episode, as in lines 24, 25, 26. By the time of the poem on the death of Alfred, the year 1036 in the *Chronicle,* rime, on the other hand, is structural, for it occurs only in the lines that fail to alliterate (6, 9, 13, 15, 20).

The mutual exclusion of rime and alliteration continues in later poetry, such as Layamon's *Brut.* In the later Middle English alliterative poetry this practice is continued, for an attempt is made to restore alliteration to its place of honor as the sole binding force of the line. Since, however, there no longer is an essential relation between the alliterating syllables and the important words of the line, as is evidenced by the number of unimportant words standing in the alliterations, and since the rhythm has been smoothed out by the linguistic changes, alliterative poetry yielded completely to rimed verse.

Tradition, therefore, played a greater role in the maintenance of the alliterative line in England than in any of the other West Germanic dialects. In early Old English, the strict Germanic line was maintained through retention of an old poetic vocabulary and syntax; in late Middle English, alliterative poetry was composed, though with linguistic rhythms totally different from those of the Germanic or Old English alliterative line. In Old English, linguistic changes had by no means removed the basis for alliterative verse; the relatively strong stress actually supported it. But as substantives gradually lost their distinctive stresses, the language with its great increase in number of function words was more adaptable to rimed than to alliterative verse, and even a strong tradition could not hinder the gradual adoption of rime.

The Rhythm of Old Saxon

Linguistic rhythm is even lighter in the continental Germanic languages. Prose texts from this area show a higher proportion of short vowels than do our Old English texts, and linguistic and metrical phenomena bear witness to a reduction of intensity of primary stresses. The Old Saxon poets had to contend with as many short syllables as did the Old English; in addition they could not rely on a strong primary stress to maintain the force of their line. As a result the rhythm of the Old Saxon poems is no longer determined primarily by metrical principles, but rather by their content. One may find lines like *Heliand* 217:

fernun gêre,   formon uuordu,
    former year   with first word

which seem to indicate a mastery over the rhythm; others like 219:

hêtan scoldi.   That ic an mînumu hugi ni gidar
    should be called.   That I cannot in my mind

that seem to start out smoothly, but then founder into prose; and others like line 225:

Thô sprac eft the frôdo man,   the thar consta filo mahlian:
   Then spoke again the wise man,   he who well could talk:

which are quite difficult to distinguish from prose, and fit the schemes of metrists only through considerable metrical manipulation.

As in Old English we may assume from the increased number of svarabhakti vowels in Old Saxon a further reduction in the stresses of secondary syllables. Besides the weakly stressed vowels that Old Saxon, like all the West Germanic languages, had inherited in words like *accar, fugal, uuânom,* additional svarabhakti vowels developed, especially in the neighborhood of *r,* e.g., *skarapun* beside earlier *skarpun* 'sharp'; with *beraht,* compare Old English *beorht* 'bright', with *thuru(h),* compare Old English *þurh* 'through'. That these vowels were but weakly articulated is clear from the assimilation they undergo; as in the words cited above, the timbre of the Old Saxon svarabhakti vowels generally follows that of the primarily stressed vowels of the word. Even inherited vowels of weakly stressed syllables underwent such assimilation, e.g., *jungoro* beside *jungaro* 'younger'. Such uncertainty of articulation hardly permits the assumption of strong secondary and tertiary stresses.

In Old Saxon too the reduction of secondary stresses was carried much farther than in contemporaneous Old English. Old English poets could use the secondary stresses of the second elements of some compounds in metrically prominent positions; e.g., *lîc-homa* 'body' occupies both lifts of the first half-line in *Beowulf* 812; in Old Saxon the second element of its cognate, *lîk-hamo* and similar compounds, was so weakly stressed that it never occupies the lifts in the *Heliand.* Inasmuch as these compounds formed the mainstay of some of the characteristic Germanic rhythmic types, Sievers' D and E patterns, these became much less compact in Old Saxon. In Old Norse and Old English they centered about compounds

with a second secondary following a primary stress, e.g.,
(*Vkv.* 7.4):

endlangan sal:
    along the hall

and (*Beo.* 998):

eal inneweard   īrenbendum fæst,
    all inward   fast in iron bands

But in Old Saxon the strength of these patterns was often
diminished because poets used short stressed plus weakly
stressed syllables in place of one heavily stressed; for example,
in the *Heliand* 2446, beside

man mislîco:
    men variously:

we find in lines 1007 and 4437 for the pattern $\acute{\ }\ \acute{\ }\grave{\ }$ x

manno mêndâdi
    the evil deeds of men

manno thea minniston
    the lowest of men

and even, in line 2806,

manno thene mâreostan
    the most famous of men

Such relaxation of rhythm is not found generally in Old English alliterative verse until the twelfth century.

It is also evident in the poetic vocabulary that the stress
pattern in compounds, the feature which distinguished them
from adjectival phrases, was weakened early in Old Saxon.
Old English alliterative poetry is rich in compounds, many
of which are nowhere else attested; such compounds are even
found in the later Old English works, e.g., the *Judith,* and in
the Middle English alliterative poems. Old Saxon has rela-

105

tively few, and almost none that do not occur elsewhere; their place is taken by phrasal constructions.

Among the great number of compounds in our Germanic writings, those whose members alliterate are characteristically limited to verse. Since they are not found at all in prose, and rather uncommonly in verse, Schröder[10] suggested that they were nonce compounds, created by a poet for a particular line; in this way the *Beowulf* poet had used the compound *gold-wine* 'gold-friend' five times, and then in line 2652 we find a new compound:

mid mīnne goldgyfan   glēd fæðmię.
    with my gold-giver   gleed should enfold.

Old Saxon poetry, on the other hand, contains few compounds whose components alliterate, the *Heliand* only one in every 350 lines. Even these Schröder assumes were taken over by the poet from a poem which had not come down to us, for they are restricted in occurrence to certain parts of the poem, and are not particularly apposite for the lines in which they occur. The lack of such poetic creations may well be the result of the linguistic changes; for if the structure of old compounds like *līkhamo* had been obscured in Old Saxon by the reduction of a strong secondary stress, the *Heliand* poet would have had no pattern on which to construct new ones.

But our Old Saxon writings do not merely attest a reduction of secondary stress; they also give evidence of a loss in intensity of primary word stress. For in Old Saxon poetic rhythm, sentence stress comes to predominate over word stress. In Old English verse, words which were commonly used in the metrically prominent syllables of a line are rarely found elsewhere, especially not in less prominent positions; their word stress would have been too strong to be tolerated in such positions of the line. In the *Heliand,* on the other

[10] *ZfdA,* 43 (1899), 361–85.

hand, one can find in less prominent positions numerous words which commonly stand in the most prominent metrical positions; e.g., *gōd* 'good' in the *Beowulf* alliterates in 33 out of 35 occurrences, in the *Heliand* in only 88 out of 155. This fluctuation is possible because the rhythm is no longer determined by word stress, but rather by sentence stress, which is an element of sentence intonation and correlates primarily with the meaning of the line rather than with the stress of word-classes. Hence classes of words, such as the verbs, which previously had been avoided in the positions of chief metrical prominence, are used in them more and more commonly. The *Genesis* went a step farther, using such words in accented alliterating positions even in lines which laid no special rhetorical stress on them, for example (lines 243–46),

Thuo ni *dorste* Abraham leng   drohtin sînan
furður frâgon,   hac he fell im after te bedu
an kneo craftag;   *quað* he gerno
is geld gereuuedi   endi gode theonodi,
    Then not longer could Abraham   that lord of his
    further question,   but he fell down to prayer
    on powerful knee;   with pleasure he spoke,
    got ready his offering   and God served,

Since the *Genesis* author has not lost all the techniques of Germanic poetry—for example, the mastery of dialogue—it seems reasonable to conclude from lines like 243 that the change in stress, not lack of ability or technique, brought about such a departure from traditional alliterative practice.

    A further change in alliterative technique supports the assumption that alliterating syllables had lost much of their relative force; for initial consonants no longer seem adequate to bind the alliterative line. Vowels in the alliterating syllables of Old Saxon poetry rime in one of every three alliterating words, in sharp contrast to northern verse where it was con-

sidered erroneous to rime them. Not only the initial *h* but also
the following *e* agree in *Heliand* 3002:

hebbian te iro hêrron :   im is helpono tharf,
    have for their master :   to them help is needed,

Compare also (lines 817, 1529, 3912, and 5635) :

bihuuî gio sô kindisc man   sulica quiði mahti
    why a man so young   might make such statements
sô hue sô ôgon genimid   ôðres mannes,
    whoever an eye might take   from an other man,
sô hue sô thar mid thurstu   bithuungan uuâri,
    as many as there by thirst   tormented might be,
faðmon gifastnot :   'fader alomahtig', quathie
    fastened in his arms :   'Father Almighty', said he

Because of the frequency of such "extended alliterations" one
can hardly avoid the conclusion that the Old Saxon poets
felt a need to call special attention to their binding elements.
In England such alliterations are not commonly found until
the period of medieval alliterative verse.

    Coupled with the decrease in strength of the primary
stress was an increase in the number of light syllables. The
over-all proportion of heavy syllables is markedly less than
that of Old English. In one of the few prose documents that
have come down to us, the Old Saxon *Confession of Faith,*
two out of every five syllables are short; in a fragment of a
homily of Bede the proportion is even higher, as indicated
by the following table:

	CoF	*HoB*
⏑	60	133
⏑C	65	97
⏑CC	8	9
—	16	64
—C	3	11

The Old English poets for a long time avoided the changes

of rhythm caused by the increase of weakly stressed syllables through the employment of a poetic vocabulary which was quite distinct from that of prose. But in North Germany social conditions seem no longer to have favored a transmission of an old poetic vocabulary; as a result the rhythm of poetry was based on that of prose and the great number of light syllables could not be avoided.

Sievers long ago pointed out a distinctive Old Saxon use of polysyllables that he ascribed to Old Saxon linguistic developments.[11] In Old Saxon, forms like *sundiono, gimarcode, aleskidin, hêtana, mînaro,* were permitted to stand at the end of a line in opposition to the commonly observed practice of restricting the final drop to one syllable. This innovation Sievers ascribed to the rise of many forms with a weekly stressed middle vowel.[12] The *Heliand* poet made a few attempts to employ such words in the traditional patterns, for we find occasional lines, as 3671, of the type

Thô nâhide   neriendo Crist
    Then came nearer   Christ the Savior

but these seem excessively light in the *Heliand,* as one may note from the very next line

the gôdo te Hierusalem.   Quam imu thar tegegnes filu
    the good to Jerusalem.   Came then to greet him many

Since uses of words like *nâhide* with two metrical stresses are rare in comparison with uses in lines like 5394

uuitan, huat sia uuarahtun.   Thiu uurd nâhida thuo,
    know what they worked.   The wyrd then approached,

we must assume that the poet found the second stress on these words excessively weak.

In Old Saxon the frequency of light syllables can easily

[11] *PBB,* 5 (1878), 82–89.
[12] See also *PBB,* 12 (1887), 286-87.

be understood upon examination of the linguistic changes which Old Saxon underwent. As pointed out above, many svarabhakti vowels arose, all of which were short; these contributed further to lightness by opening preceding syllables. Other shortenings must be deduced from linguistic developments, for quantity of vowels is rarely marked in our Old Saxon documents; we have evidence of this type for shortening of the stem vowel in preterite forms like *fell, held, weld, et*.

But again the greatest cause of lightening the weight of the line is the increase in pronouns, adverbs, and other weakly stressed words that are avoided in earlier alliterative verse. Most of the absurdly long lines of Old Saxon poetry abound in such function words, for example (lines 1494 and 5964):

suâs man an saca :   than ne sî he imu eo sô suuîðo an sibbiun
                                                                bilang,

a close friend in sin :   than no matter how near he is to
                                                    him in kinship,

uuas im thoh an iro gisîðie samad   endi frâgoda umbi huilica
                                                    sia saca sprâkin :

he was nonetheless together with them   and asked about
                                            what things they were speaking :

Function words were apparently so difficult to avoid that the *Genesis* poet almost developed a rhythmical formula for them; the second half-line of about one of every thirty of his lines consists of an infinitive plus modal auxiliary, for example (lines 210*b*, 237*b*, and 305*b*):

haldan uuille.
    will hold.
sittian muotin,
    might be located,

libbian uueldin.
    wished to live.

These patterns furnished a surprisingly weak close to the line.

But the chief device used to accommodate the many function words, and also to uphold the weight of the line, was the expanded line. The *Heliand* contains a much higher proportion of these than does the *Beowulf,* and permits in them the same relative increase over the Old English line as it does in the normal lines. In other respects, the two dialects agree in the use of expanded lines; in Old Saxon too they are found in groups and are limited to passages of elevated or high emotional content, such as the following lines (1308–12) from the Sermon on the Mount:

frôfre an iro frâhon rîkia.   Sâlige sind ôc, the sie hîr frumono
                                        gilustid,
rincos, that sie rehto adômien.   Thes môtun sie uuerðan an
                                   them rîkia drohtines
gifullit thurh iro ferhton dâdi :   sulîcoro môtun sie frumono
                                     bicnêgan,
thie rincos, thie hîr rehto adômiad,   ne uuilliad an rûnun
                                     besuuîcan
man, thar sie at mahle sittiad.
    comfort in their Lord's kingdom.   Blessed are also, those
                                 who here long after good,
    heroes, that they perfectly judge.   Therefore in the presence of God they may be
    perfected through their pious deeds :   such favor they may attain,
    the heroes, who here truly judge,   who do not wish to betray in secret
    the men, when they sit at the judgment.

And as in Old English, the expanded lines are less irregular in rhythm than are the normal verses, for example, *Beowulf* 2996

111

mon on middangearde,   syððan hīe ðā mǣrða geslōgon;
men in the middle-planet,   since they there made their
name;

One can virtually read this line, like some of those in the *Heliand* passage cited above, in the alternating rhythm of the later rimed verse.

That the Old Saxon linguistic changes led to regularity of rhythm can possibly most strikingly be demonstrated by citing the suggestion of a German scholar, Trautmann, that the *Heliand* was actually a translation from Old English.[13] In support of his suggestion Trautmann rewrote some of the *Heliand*'s aberrant lines in Old English to illustrate that they there would fit the requirements of alliterative verse. Such are:

3145a	glîtandi glîmo	OE	glīdende glǣm
1186a	nettiu endi neglid-scipu	OE	net ond nægled scipu
2920a	an them sêe uppan	OE	an þǣm sǣ uppan

Almost all of the Old Saxon words that Trautmann replaces, *glîmo, nettiu, endi, sêe,* lead to an alternating rhythm. But not all of Trautmann's objections were to lines that were too long in Old Saxon. Some were too short, again because of linguistic changes, e.g.,

1916b	managa sind thero	OE	monge sind þāra
1698a	mênful maco	OE	mānful macige

Even in these lines the linguistic developments had led to alternating rhythm. After these rhythmic changes had been brought about, all that was required for a change from alliterative to rimed verse was the introduction of rime and the reduction of alliteration to a stylistic feature.

Since our two Old Saxon poems were composed in the same tradition, they show no marked difference of poetic form, and both follow the patterns of the colloquial. Their rhythm, therefore, differs considerably from that of Old Eng-

---

[13] M. Trautmann, *Bonner beiträge zur anglistik* 17 (1905), 123 ff.

lish, as may be noted from the observation first made by Rieger, and in greater detail by Sievers, before the Old Saxon *Genesis* was known to exist, that a section of the Old English *Genesis* was translated from Old Saxon; even in a translation the Old English poet was unable to conceal the more diffuse rhythm of Old Saxon. Linguistic changes had contributed both a weaker stress and a greater number of weakly stressed syllables. In maintaining alliterative verse, the Old Saxon poets introduced various modifications, chiefly a longer line, and they developed a straggling line that is characteristically Old Saxon.

The Rhythm of Old High German

Thirty years after the *Heliand* was composed rime was introduced as an innovation by Otfrid. Unfortunately, we have no Old Saxon poetry written after the *Heliand* and *Genesis,* so we cannot determine how the Old Saxon poets would have solved their problems in form. By comparing the process of development in Old High German verse we may assume that Old Saxon too would have turned to rimed verse with its reliance on stress alone rather than on stress coupled with quantity and its alternating rather than sharply irregular rhythm. For although the Old High German prose rhythm differs considerably from that of Old Saxon, it too could not readily be accommodated to alliterative verse. The last Old High German alliterative poem that has come down to us, the *Muspilli,* contains as many rhythmical aberrancies as does the Old Saxon poetry and is as relaxed in form, even though it does not stand in the Old English epic tradition but rather in the stricter tradition of the short and compact ode. The

113

linguistic changes had made Old High German even less suitable for alliterative poetry than was Old Saxon.

Like the other West Germanic languages Old High German had a preponderance of short syllables, as illustrated in the following analysis of a passage from *Isidor* 6, and *Tatian*, Luke 2: 1–7:

	Isidor	Tatian
◡	88	101
◡C	60	79
◡CC	6	8
—	14	26
—C	17	10

In Old High German there was no syncopation of unstressed syllables that might have contributed to the quality of preceding syllables. The direct contrary can be observed. Unstressed syllables maintained their length, while stressed syllables continued short; as a result some lines of the *Muspilli* have short syllables in metrically prominent positions, long in nonprominent, for example (lines 64a and 92),

daz er rahôno uuelîha
    that he every revenge
alero lido uuelîhc   unzi in den luzîgun vinger,
    every single member   up to his small finger,

Since even the few long syllables that Old High German maintained often lacked the chief stress, the two components of the alliterative rhythm conflicted with each other: the *Muspilli* poet, disregarding quantity, chose stress as the determining factor of his rhythm, and, in this way, had already adopted the rhythmic principles of rimed verse.

Though the rhythm of Old High German was light because of the preponderance of short syllables we have no evidence of a strong primary stress on the first syllable of words, as in Old Norse and Old English, which might have upheld

114

to some extent the alliterative rhythm. The very preservation
of the long weakly stressed syllables points to a fairly even distribution of the articulatory energy; compare with Old Saxon
guldin and Old English *gylden* Old High German *guldîn*
'golden' where the quantity of a weakly stressed vowel was
preserved, or with Old Saxon *gibunden* Old High German
gibuntan 'bound' where the quality was preserved. In Old
High German, as in Old Saxon, sentence stress predominates
over word stress, and can elevate any word to the highest position in the rhythm. In *Muspilli* 79

> denne varant engilâ   uper dio marhâ
>   then angels proceed   over the region

the preposition *uper* has greater stress than has *marhâ*.

A linguistic analysis of Old High German then shows
that the language has neither the quantity nor the strong
stress necessary to maintain alliterative verse. Equally dis-
astrous for its maintenance was the increase in the number
of function words. In a line like *Muspilli* 63

> pidiu ist demo manno so guot,   denner ze demo mahale quimit,
>   therefore it is so good for a man   when he goes to the
>   judgment

over half of the material is made up of conjunctions, adverbs,
and articles. In an attempt to find in the *Muspilli* a semblance
of alliterative verse, one of the editors, Müllenhoff, deleted
some of these; he revised line 63 to read

> pidiu ist demo manne guot,   denne er zu mahale quimit,

But as a later editor, Steinmeyer, pointed out, such attempts
are hopeless. For the poem abounds in function words, and
Müllenhoff could not begin to remove all of them; he deleted
denne in three lines, kept it in others, deleted *pidiu* once, but
elsewhere, as in line 63, left it.

Müllenhoff's attempts at emendation even yielded an

example of how the *Muspilli* poet subordinated rhythmic to syntactic patterns. In line 76

daz ist allaz sô pald,   daz imo nioman kipâgan ni mak.
  all of that is so bold,   that no one can combat it.

Müllenhoff deleted the second *daz* in the interests of a more normal alliterative rhythm, changing 76*b* to a main clause.[14] But Steinmeyer observed that in the *Muspilli* verbs stand at the end of subordinate clauses, not main clauses, and therefore this *daz* cannot be elided. It follows that the poet is more rigorous in observing syntactic than metrical patterns. Since Müllenhoff was unable to eliminate "metrical errors" from the poem, we must conclude that the poet himself, not a scribe, was responsible for them, and that they reflect the extent to which linguistic developments had made impossible Old High German alliterative verse.

Possibly the poorest line stands at the end of a short episode which the poet lifted from elsewhere, line 60:

uuâr ist denne diu marha,   dâr man dâr eo mit sînen mâgon
                                 piehc?
  where now is the field,   where one formerly with his
                                 kinsmen battled?

Since this line stands at the end of this episode, is written in the form of a question, and in no way rises above the mediocrity of the poem, I consider it and the following lines some of the few written by the poet who constructed the *Muspilli*. The poet continues by answering his question in the only rimed couplet of the poem:

diu marha ist farprunnan,   diu sêla stêt pidungan,
ni uueiz mit uuiu puaze: sô verit si za uuîze.
  The field is burned,   the soul is constrained,
  knows not with what penance: thus it goes to sentence.

[14] See *Denkmäler deutscher Poesie und Prosa aus dem VIII–XII Jh.*, ed. E. Steinmeyer (3d ed., Berlin, 1892), 2, 40.

These lines might easily fit into Otfrid's poem. When the unfortunate *Muspilli* poet found he was to write some lines of his own, he used both the rhythm and the type of cadence that Otfrid chose.

In the interpolated section which precedes, lines 60–62, we can note the shifts in sentence rhythm which led to the introduction of rime. Early Germanic poetry would have been quite unfavorable for the introduction of end rime because the last part of the line was stressed to a lesser degree than the preceding section. But in lines 37–59 of the *Muspilli* we find a high proportion of alliterations on the fourth beat of the line, a proportion of almost one in three, or even higher if we leave out of account the reasonably well-written Sibylline lines 50–56, an interpolation inside the larger interpolation. Compare lines 57–59:

dar ni mac denne mak andremo helfan vora demo muspille.
denne daz preita uuasal allaz varprinnit,
enti vuir enti luft iz allaz arfurpit,

  there one kinsman another cannot from the judgment
               keep.

  for the broad rain everything burns,
  both fire and air sweeps away everything,

The shift from a reliance on word stress to sentence stress apparently led to a stress on the fourth main beat of the line which equaled or surpassed that of the third; as a result it was as compelling to alliterate this beat as to alliterate the third. It may be worth noting that one of the few alliterating lines in Otfrid also alliterates the second word in the second half-line, I:5.11:

Wáhero dúacho werk wírkento
  Of winsome clothes working the work

The way from the structure of lines 57–59 to that of 61–62 was simple. While the *Muspilli* poet just ventures briefly into

117

the new form, Otfrid adopts it deliberately, introducing but few examples of the old alliterative rhythm.

Baesecke has further demonstrated how the change from the two stresses per half-line to the four of the new "half-line" may be inferred from irregular lines of the *Muspilli*. Line 39*b* is an impossible alliterative half-line with its anacrusis of seven syllables and its choice of alliterating stressed syllables: *denne uuirdit untar in uuîc arhapan.* If one, however, assumes stresses on *uuirdit* and *untar* as well the line gains shape, though only in the new rhythm. As Baesecke puts it, the poet of this section of the *Muspilli* has gently glided into the new art form.

Otfrid tells us explicitly in his prefaces the models for his form and his binding element—rime. Study of the *Muspilli* shows how the linguistic developments made the alliterative form unsuitable and almost forced the adoption of the new form. Our chief interest in Otfrid's poem here is to note how he gradually improved his technique, eliminating irregularities in both rime and rhythm.

Those parts of the first book which Otfrid wrote earliest contain his greatest irregularities. Alliterating lines remind us of his pioneering in rime. For some unaccountable reason Otfrid did not replace these when he revised his poem; one may have survived because it was a well-known sermon tag (I.18.9):

thar is líb ana tód,   líoht ana fínstri,
    there is life without death,   light without darkness.

It is found in the *Muspilli,* too, line 14.

Otfrid's experiments and rime improvements, leading to the inclusion of rimes beginning with the stressed syllables, have been discussed in Chapter 2. As noted there the last sections of the poem provide him with no troubles in his riming. Otfrid's efforts to regulate his rhythm are less readily accessible to us. Brinkmann, however, pointed out one line that preserves a record of Otfrid's struggles with rhythm.[15] The very next line after this alliterative one illustrates how Otfrid changed from the alliterative to the alternating rhythm. In one manuscript the half-line I.18.10 reads

éngilo kúnni   (joh éwinigo wúnni.)
    the tribe of angels   (and eternal joy.) ;

in the other

éngillichaz kúnni
    the angelic tribe.

The change from a noun in the genitive to an adjective smoothed out the line, bringing it into uniformity with the new rhythm.

As the rimes increase in extent, they affect the rhythm more and more. The American scholar Holzwarth[16] has pointed out that the lines with the greatest proportion of imperfect rimes are those in which the two half-lines differ in rhythm, for example (I.5.3),

Tho quam bóto fona góte,   éngil ir hímile,
    Then came from God a messenger,   from heaven an
                                     angel,

As the rimes are extended, the rhythm is leveled out (III. 14.81) :

Want ér ist selbo wúnno   joh álles gúates brunno ;
    Since he all pleasure brings,   and from him all good
                                     springs ;

Otfrid's adoption of rime therefore helped him to level the rhythm further.

A comparison of Otfrid's writings with the other Old

[15] *AfdA*, 66 (1937), 3–12, especially 10.
[16] Charles H. Holzwarth, *Zu Otfrids Reim* (Borna–Leipzig, R. Noske, 1909).

119

High German rimed poems supports the contention that Otfrid's rhythm was provided for him by the language. For the
other rimed poems agree with Otfrid's in rhythm, if not in
rime. Stylistic studies indicate that there was no mutual influence between these poets and Otfrid; we can, therefore,
ascribe the peculiar agreement in their skill with rhythm and
rime to the one common influence, the Old High German
language.

Although Otfrid and the other Old High German poets
had turned from the requirements of alliterative poetry to
those of rimed verse, they did not abandon the freedoms of
alliterative verse. The number of syllables in a rime was not
fixed; weakly stressed syllables were unregulated both in anacrusis and the drops of the line, though the Old High German poets never allowed the number of weakly stressed syllables in either position that are common in the late alliterative
poets. These freedoms were not abandoned until the time of
classical Middle High German verse. Their abandonment,
while not brought about by linguistic changes, conforms closely
to these. For between Old High German and Middle High
German, vowels in weakly stressed syllables were generally reduced to *e;* and in trisyllabic words, both long and short vowels were syncopated in positions of weakest stress. Old High
German *heilag* 'holy' shows up as Middle High German
heilec, Old High German *hôhiro, hôhoro* as Middle High
German *hœher* 'higher', Old High German *demu, demo* 'the'
as Middle High German *deme;* the syncopated forms of the
trisyllables fit the alternating rhythm, e.g., Old High German
sâlida, Middle High German *sælde* 'blessing', Old High German *bezzisto,* Middle High German *beste* 'best', Old High
German *wartêta,* Middle High German *wartte* 'waited', Old
High German *uuuntarôn,* Middle High German *uundern*
'wonder'. In this way some of the rhythmic difficulties that
faced Otfrid were lost by the time of Gottfried.

Middle High German rhythm, after these linguistic changes, was essentially like that of modern German. It was determined almost solely by accent; the various linguistic changes had virtually removed rhythmic distinctions based on quantity. Some of these survived in Middle High German, especially in the rimes. The poets distinguished between rimes with long stem syllables, e.g., *recken,* and those with short stem syllables, e.g., *degen,* classing the latter with the monosyllabic masculine rimes, e.g., *stât.* Yet the distinction was not observed without exception; one sometimes has the impression that the poets maintained it by convention, rather than because of the stress patterns of the language.

Changes after the classical Middle High German period leveled out completely the quantity of syllables; short vowels in open syllables were lengthened, such as the *a* in *name* 'name', while long vowels in closed syllables were shortened, as the *â* in *brâht* 'brought'. After syllabic quantity was leveled, German poetic and linguistic rhythms were determined solely by the stress.

The abandonment of the alliterative line in Old High German can, accordingly, be ascribed in great part to linguistic developments. Primary stresses were light; the number of weakly stressed short syllables was great. Prose rhythm alone must have suggested to Otfrid the advantages of rimed over alliterative verse.

The Poetic Rhythms and the Linguistic Changes

All the Germanic dialects show a clear relation between their linguistic changes and the development of verse form. We have suggested above that each dialect had inherited the same poetic form from Proto-Germanic; each modified this form as it underwent linguistic changes, until the alliterative line became characteristically different in the several areas.

Primarily affected by the linguistic changes was the form of the individual lines, not at all that of extended forms. In the northern dialects the number of weakly accented syllables was reduced; the alliterative lines were shortened accordingly, and contained a minimum of drops. In the West Germanic languages, on the other hand, the number of weakly stressed syllables was increased, and the alliterative line was correspondingly extended, chiefly by an increase in the number of drops.

The linguistic changes did not, however, hold absolute sway over poetic forms; when they did not affect the phonological features characterizing a segment of poetic form, they could be held in abeyance—as in the early Old English poetry —by the maintenance of traditional patterns. For the Old English linguistic changes had affected only one of the two phonological features underlying the alliterative form; the balance between strongly stressed and weakly stressed syllables had been disturbed by the rise of a number of new weakly stressed syllables, but, on the other hand, the weight of the strong stress was maintained. By retention of traditional patterns, such as nominal compounds, paratactic rather than hypotactic constructions, and few sentence connectives, lines were written in Old English which contained as few unaccented syllables as did Old Icelandic poetry, and were equally heavy.

In the continental West Germanic languages both features of the alliterative rhythm were affected by linguistic changes: primary word stress was weakened, and the number of weakly stressed syllables increased. Consequently, the alliterative line became shapeless, scarcely distinguishable from prose, and was abandoned in favor of verse with end rime.

England likewise adopted end-rime verse when poetic traditions no longer maintained stock elements of alliterative verse, such as the nominal compounds, and when sentence stress became more prominent than word stress. End-rime verse, with its even rhythm, accorded much better than alliterative verse with languages that had shifted the predominant stress from specific classes of words, notably the substantives, to specific positions in the sentence, leveling at the same time the differences between the stresses on individual words.

Study of the poetic changes in the various old Germanic dialects suggests then that linguistic form determined poetic form. When the features underlying a poetic form, however, had not been completely modified by phonological changes, artificial or traditional patterns could maintain poetic forms that were no longer in agreement with the predominant phonological features of a language.

4 AUDIENCE, PRESENTATION, AND CHANGE IN VERSE FORM

With the linguistic changes that the various Germanic languages undergo we can account for the changes in rhythm in the individual lines. In Old Norse, where words were shortened through the loss of weakly stressed vowels, the proportion of long vowels and heavy syllables increased, but since the accent was emphatic, a few syllables satisfied the requirements of the alliterative rhythm, and alliterative poetry was maintained. In the West Germanic languages, on the other hand, as a result of the linguistic changes discussed in the preceding chapter, the alliterative line was progressively abandoned in favor of the more gently accented rimed lines which the Germanic poets learned to know from Latin poetry.

While the changes in language rhythm determined the developments in the individual lines, they did not bring about changes in extended forms. It may be more accurate to speak of the introduction of extended forms, for in old Germanic poetry we can hardly speak of a unit of poetic form longer than the individual line. The repetition of similar patterns as in the charms may have led to the effect of continuity beyond a whole line, e.g., the Merseburg charm, or *Song of Weland* stanza 34 cited above; but each repeated line was always complete in itself and the omission of one would scarcely have merited notice unless the number was determined by non-formal, such as magical, principles. Later Germanic poetry, however, strives for extended forms, and these differ greatly in their refinement and smoothness of rhythm from the old Germanic poetry.

In the north, alliterative lines were grouped in stanzas consisting of two, four, or even more long lines. The skalds restricted the stanza even further, limiting those of a favorite verse form, the *dróttkvætt,* to eight half-lines. In the interest of solemnity stanzas might be further grouped together, as in the Skaldic *drápa* with its *stef* or refrain. But this was the only formal bond in the solemn *drápa.* It was not an element of the art of even the form-conscious skalds to repeat formal elements, such as alliterative patterns from stanza to stanza, somewhat as rime schemes are repeated in modern forms like the Spenserian stanza, or to maintain one rhythmic pattern for similar parts of successive stanzas. Both in alliteration and in rhythm each line of an alliterative poem was independent and remained independent as long as alliterative poetry was maintained.

In the south two types of extended form were introduced and widely adopted: the long epic, in eighth-century England, from where it spread to the continent; and the Romance lyric, four centuries later.

As in the Homeric poems or the *Aeneid,* the longer elements in epic poetry were determined by syntactic, stylistic, and narrative, not by prosodic criteria; prosodically each line of the epics composed in the alliterative form maintained its independence. Prosodic units extending beyond the long line were introduced only in the rimed epic poetry, as in Otfrid's *Krist,* with its thoroughgoing pairing of two long lines, each divided by rime into half-lines.

In the twelfth century the southern lyric poetry developed an even greater variety of stanzaic forms than had the Skaldic. Stanza forms in the southern lyric could differ in number of lines, in the length and rhythm of lines, and in distribution of rime. Yet in this poetry, too, we note a limit on form. Though poets, for example Walther von der Vogelweide, often compose poems consisting of a number of stanzas in the same form, the individual stanzas usually preserve their autonomy; as a result editors sometimes have difficulties deciding what is the proper order of the stanzas or whether stanzas in the same form belong together in "one poem," and manuscripts frequently omit stanzas or present varying arrangements. Accordingly, we may note parallelisms, and contrasts, between the northern Skaldic and the southern lyric verse. In the south the rhythmical parallels between stanzas of one poem are much greater than in the Skaldic verse; for in the southern lyric, rhythmical patterns in one line of a stanza may be repeated exactly in the corresponding line of another. Skaldic poetry demands only a likeness in the number of syllables, but does not regulate the distribution of stresses. Skaldic verse, on the other hand, requires a regular extent of line with stanzas consisting of a succession of either six, eight, four, etc. syllables. Stanzas in the south require almost the converse. With these differences in execution the two schools strove for perfection in external form. When imperfections were introduced by masters of either form they were deliberate and purposed. In the poem which alludes to Atze, Walther von der Vogelweide's *e* : *ä* rimes defer to a Thuringian audience that did not distinguish these vowels;[1] the skald Thorgils used quantitatively imperfect rimes in his lines when he was competing with his king, for he perhaps felt it unwise to triumph over him.[2]

We find these extended forms among social groups that arose in the Germanic world after the eighth century: the long epic was introduced in the English monasteries; Skaldic poetry flourished in the halls of the Viking rulers; the south-

---

[1] Kraus, *Die Gedichte Walthers von der Vogelweide*, 82.11, 115.
[2] Hollander, *The Skalds*, 202–205.

ern love lyric and minnesong in the medieval chivalric courts. In these new cultural groups not only new poetic forms were introduced but also new methods of presentation. The Old High German monk Otfrid composed his epic for a reading audience; the tenth-century skald Egil is described as reciting his *drápa,* much as would any modern poet; the thirteenth-century German minnesingers presented their poems to the accompaniment of melodies which they themselves had composed. Other genres, and other ages, favored different modes of presentation. During the six centuries of early Germanic verse that we are concerned with, the changing audiences were introduced to their poetry variously, by eye, by ear, with or without the accompaniment of music.

In spite of several reports on the presentation of Germanic poetry before the eighth century we do not know definitely how it was presented, whether sung to the accompaniment of a harp, chanted with introductory chords, or recited without musical accompaniment. Contemporary sources suggest the use of a harp, e.g., Cassiodorus who describes the presenter of poetry (in France to be sure, and accordingly possibly not Germanic poetry) as singing with mouth and hands working in harmony (*Ore manibusque consona voce cantando*). Internal evidence in the languages provides no help in deciding among these possibilities, for the various terms that were later used to distinguish between song and recitation are not so used in our earliest documents; the cognates of *sing* and *song,* for example, are used both by Wulfila in our oldest Germanic material and by Otfrid five centuries later of elevated speech as well as of singing. Compare Wulfila's translation of Luke 4:16: *jah qam in Nazaraiþ, þarei was fodiþs, jah galaiþ inn bi biuhta seinamma in daga sabbato in swnagogein jah usstoþ siggwan bokos.* "And he came to Nazareth, where he had been brought up: and, as his custom was, he went into the synagogue on the sabbath day, and stood up for to read." Here *siggwan* translates Greek *an-agnōnai* 'read'. Similarly, when Otfrid speaks of the Old Testament "singing" of Christ, the word obviously means report (I.8.26) :

thie búah fon imo síngent,   wioz fórasagon zéllent.
the books of him report,   as the prophets it narrate.

When, on the other hand, the *Beowulf* poet describes the entertainment at Heorot with the words (89*b*–90*a*)

þǣr wæs hearpan swēg,
swutol sang scopes.
there was harp music,
the sweet song of the scop.

we can hardly interpret the words differently from those of Cassiodorus. This song of the scop dealing with the creation, while depicting the incidents of Genesis 1, may have been similar to the old sections of the Old Norse *Vǫluspa*, if we can accept this *Beowulf* passage as attesting to the court entertainments at the sixth-century Danish royal hall, or to Caedmon's *Song of the Creation,* if we prefer to assume that the passage refers to eighth-century English verse.

Only the prehistoric Germanic songs were accompanied by music. The genres that we know from the various dialects —the long epics, the epic lays, the Eddic and Skaldic verse— must have been recited, in spite of some suggestions to the contrary, as recently Pope[3] who believes that the Germanic like the Serbian epic was presented with the aid of music. No mention is made in manuscripts or contemporary accounts of accompaniment by the harp or by any other instrument. It is almost inconceivable that irregularity such as that found in the *Heliand* could have arisen if any accompaniment had been designed for the epic. While we have only such irregularity of form and the term "fits" (reading selections) on which to

[3] Pope, *The Rhythm of Beowulf,* 88–95.

base our assumption that the *Heliand* was not meant to be sung, Otfrid thirty years later specifically states in his preface to Liutbert that his poem is to be read. Since the *Heliand*, and Otfrid as well, stand in the tradition of the Old English epics, it is unlikely that these were to be presented differently.

Certainly the epics are less suitable for presentation with musical accompaniment than are the Skaldic poems. Concerning the presentation of these we have contemporary accounts, of which the most dramatic is the report in the *Egils saga* of Egil's recital of "Hǫfuðlausn" at the court of Eric. The saga makes no mention of a harp, describing Egil's presentation as follows :[4]

Ok er konungr hafði þetta mælt, þá gekk Egill fyrir hann ok hóf upp kvæðit ok kvað hatt ok fekk þegar hljóð:
> And when the king had said this, then Egil went before him and began his poem, and he spoke loudly, and at once all were attentive.

After the poem is presented, the text of the saga continues :

Eiríkr konungr sat uppréttr, meðan Egill kvað kvæðit, ok hvessti augun á hann ; ok er lokit var drápunni, þá mælti konungr :
> King Eric sat upright, while Egil spoke his poem, and fixed his eyes on him ; and when the drápa was completed, then the king said :

Old Norse *kveða,* which is found in both passages, is not used of singing, only of speaking, sometimes solemn speaking. Accordingly the Skaldic poems must have been recited, not sung. If now we assume a continuous tradition between the Germanic songs of praise and the Skaldic poems, we may have to reckon with the abandonment of the harp at some point. On the other hand, it is possible that, as in contemporary poetry, only some Germanic genres were sung, and that the Germanic precursors of the Skaldic occasional poems were

---

[4] *Egils saga Skalla-grímssonar* (Reykjavik, 1945), sec. 60, 200, and sec. 61, 204.

among the genres not presented to the accompaniment of the harp.

Whether or not there was a change in method of presentation between the Germanic period and the time of the dialects, we have no doubts about such a change in ninth-century Germany—a change from recitation to reading. Besides stating that his poem is designed to be read, as mentioned above, Otfrid arranged it in sections which are similar in extent to the lectionaries of the Bible. Several hundred years later, in England, Layamon too addresses the reader (I.3–4):

Nu bidded Layamon:
   alcne æðele mon.
for þene almite godd:
   þet þeos boc rede.
     Now biddeth Layamon
       every high-born man
     before the Almighty God
       who this book might read.

Even earlier alliterative poems, such as those in the *Anglo-Saxon Chronicle* and as the late Old English epics, can only have been designed to be read. After the ninth century, longer literary works were not transmitted by word of mouth in the southern Germanic area; in the north, however, neither the poems nor the prose sagas were preserved by other than oral tradition for another several hundred years.

Lyric poetry was not written down until the thirteenth century even in the south. As a result we have only a few examples of the lyric poetry popular before the time of the minnesingers. And though we have their poems in excellent parchment manuscripts prepared shortly after their death, transmission by word of mouth has cost us their melodies. Only a few manuscripts contain melodies at all; for an intelligible presentation of the melodies of minnesong we are forced to rely on the Provençal documents.

Like the lyric poetry of the minnesingers and their predecessors, which was presented orally, the medieval epics were recited to their audience. In contrast to the earlier audiences in monasteries, the courtly audiences prided themselves on their inability to read; and whether or not we accept Wolfram's assertion, *Parzival* 115.27 ff., that he himself was illiterate, his sense of humor was not quite so perverse that he could have made this bald statement to a reading audience. At the English as well as at the German courts oral presentation was the fashion; this fashion persisted until the middle classes replaced the courtly group as the chief patrons of literature; only then did poets again "indite" rather than recite their works.

We may assume, then, that the earliest Germanic poetry was presented orally, probably to the accompaniment of a harp. In the north, poetry continued to meet its audience through the ear, though without musical accompaniment. But the poetry of the south that has come down to us was designed primarily for a reading public from the ninth century onward and secondarily for recital to an illiterate audience. After the twelfth century, though, it was once again presented orally—the lyric to the accompaniment of music.

In addition to the changes in presentation, the later audiences differed from that for old Germanic poetry. The earliest Germanic poetry was composed for a simple society with but one leisure class, whose chief energies were directed towards warfare—the men training and preserving their strength for battle, the women performing menial, auxiliary activities. Men and women joined in song, before and after battle. Whatever Germanic poetry we can reconstruct was probably designed for such occasions: songs of praise celebrated heroes of the day, as the song celebrating Beowulf's victory over

131

Grendel, *Beowulf* 874 ff., and heroic lays of a previous day, such as the song of Hengest's revenge, *Beowulf* 1063 ff.

The introduction of Christianity brought a new leisure class. Beside the warrior class arose the monastery group with its devotion to learning and contemplation. Although the new monks often attempted to maintain the old heroic lays, their ideals differed from the Germanic heroic ideals, and they found less violent story more to their taste, or it was sternly recommended to them; Alcuin, for example, requested the Bishop of Lindisfarne in 797 to have Christian readings substituted for pagan poetry during mealtime entertainment.[5] The literature composed by poets of the new leisure class conformed to its tastes, whether these were formed voluntarily or by request. Yet the old literature and ideals remained firmly seated among the lay audience. Heroic lays that were popular with the Germanic warrior group were maintained by oral tradition for hundreds of years, such as the Low German ballad of Dietrich von Bern which we know only from a printed version of the sixteenth century.

The monastery audience, however, found its ideal literary matter in the Latin writings, those dealing with both pagan and Christian story. Unlike their ancestors they no longer gathered around the fire at night to hear their poetry recited, but they read it, usually singly, possibly in groups.[6] The patience of this audience would no longer be tried by a lay of sixty to a hundred lines; moreover, if another duty interrupted and required fulfilling, the reader could continue where he had left off when he returned to his book.

Cultural innovations also divided the Germanic audience. And the new monastic group attempted to expand the size of its literary audience as well as its religious influence. For the monks recognized the proselytizing effect of litera-

[5] The passage is quoted in O. Jänicke, "Zur deutschen Heldensage," *ZfdA*, 15 (1872), 314.
[6] See A. E. Schönbach, *ZfdA*, 42 (1898), 120–21.

ture and attempted to make use of it in their tribe as well as among their friends: the *Heliand* poet wrote his epic for the Saxons of North Germany; Otfrid his poem for the Franks. Literary genres which were originally designed for a select social class extended their range, transforming the tastes of other groups: besides the Old English religious epics a *Beowulf* was produced that presumably was designed for the descendants of the warrior group; after the medieval minnesong had developed fully among the courtly group, it was carried by Neidhardt and others to the peasant classes. The art forms which were developed by new leisure classes were transmitted to other social groups, sometimes finding complete acceptance, at other times only modifying existing forms.

Christianity was not the only force that rearranged the Germanic social structure. Growth in wealth and population made impossible the continuance of the old Germanic organization for warfare. After the sixth and seventh centuries, raids conducted by all able-bodied men of a tribe or nation— such as those described by Caesar or the mass migrations of the Goths and Vandals in the fourth, fifth, and sixth centuries—would have been unduly cumbersome. Instead, select groups, drawn primarily from the ruling families, but also from the peasants, continued the military activities of the earlier Germanic peoples. Other peasants, or possibly more exactly franklins, contented with their wealth, preferred not to risk their lives in unforeseeable danger. As a result the leisure classes of the Germanic nations were divided into warrior groups and peasant groups, each with varying periods of leisure and varying literary tastes. Inasmuch as these two groups were not in the literate tradition, as was the monastery group, our knowledge of their poetry is far from complete. From especially two areas do contemporary literary works of both groups survive: from the Scandinavian area, and from medieval Germany.

133

The warrior class in Scandinavia fostered Skaldic poetry; franklins the heroic and divine songs of the *Edda*. Chieftains maintained skalds in their entourage, often as their most daring fighters. After battles, and on other notable occasions, the skalds were expected to commemorate the valiant deeds of their lords. The following was completely masculine, as is the ring of the poems. For their allusions the skalds might draw on those materials which were elaborated in the Eddic poetry, but when they are called upon to present poetry at court they never recite the simpler songs. In manner the two genres contrast as markedly as in subject matter: the Eddic poetry, other than the gnomic, characteristically presented striking stories of Germanic gods and heroes in straightforward accounts; the Skaldic poetry characteristically depicted and glorified emotions, chiefly the valor of the princes, in extremely sophisticated verse.

By the medieval period, warfare on the continent was less desperate, almost a genteel pursuit, with splendid contests between pre-eminent heroes. Engagements were no longer hit-and-run raids. Moreover, they were much more infrequent than were the early Scandinavian battles. After contests were completed, or even as they were being carried on, the warriors had ample leisure to relax in their secure castles. Their ladies were not assigned menial chores or handicrafts, but shared the intellectual pursuits and the entertainments of the knights. Whereas in the north warfare was its own end, here it was ideally subordinated to the service of woman; combat was often undertaken merely to gain the favor of a lady. The epic poets at the court chose as subjects for their poems heroes such as the Arthurian knights who illustrated the ideals of courtly life, often dealing with the relation of love to other ideals, as in Hartmann's *Erec,* where the hero neglected his other courtly obligations in favor of the cult of love, or his *Iwein,* where the hero subordinated love unduly to his military pursuits. The lyric poets glorified the ideal emotions of the courtly class.

But in both the south and the north the leisure class of the ruling group possessed one major interest which varied with the composition of the leisure class: the predominantly male warrior group of the north concerned itself primarily with war; the more gentle courtly group of the south with love.

In the south too, a second class—that of the peasants—supported a separate literature. This compared with the poetry of the courtly class as did the Eddic with the Skaldic poetry, being unsophisticated in tone and confined largely to narrating the old heroic stories, like that of Dietrich von Bern.

Contemporaneously with the warrior and peasant groups other classes maintained their literature; but most of this is not pertinent to our study, for it was not written in a Germanic language. The leisure church groups at all times wrote Latin poetry and prose, hymns, sequences, dramas, epics, in addition to didactic literature. The dominant ruling group in England after the eleventh century favored French literature, leaving Germanic story to the peasants and possibly to the barons of the northwest when it was maintained at all. By the time Germanic literature was resumed in England, a new leisure group had arisen, the merchant class, whose literary tastes required a period of cultivation. At its height in the fourteenth century this literature incorporated as many elements from the Classical and Romance tradition as from the Germanic. The change from the Germanic ideals of form to the new form had been completed earlier, paralleling to a great extent the changes taking place in Germany, without producing notable verse in any quantity. Accordingly, we will deal primarily with verse produced in Germany, drawing parallels when pertinent to that produced in England. Changes in audience clearly determined the changes in subject matter that we find in early German literature. It is of further importance to inquire whether the shifts of audience also occasioned changes in form, by reason both of their special interests and the manner of presentation which the various audiences favored.

Two genres of Germanic poetry—minnesong and Skaldic verse—were composed for and cultivated by highly specialized audiences. The aims of both types of poetry are remarkably similar, as may be observed by comparing Günther Müller's characterization of minnesong,[7] and Hollander's of Skaldic poetry.[8] In each type personal emotion is at a minimum, and the emphasis is on emotions favored by contemporary social conventions. The social conventions of minnesong have to do with courtly ideals and courtly conduct; those of Skaldic poetry with martial ideals and martial conduct. Under these conventions are buried the personal life and feelings of poets of either school. Few of the Middle High German minnesongs give us clues about the personality of the author; judged by their content most of them might have been written by one minnesinger as well as the next. The poets writing at the end of the thirteenth century meet ladies with hearts as stony as were those of their grandmothers. Likewise the skalds produced a succession of verses clothed in kennings and stylized syntax but similar in content; eleventh-century kings fought as valiantly as their ancestors in the ninth.

In both schools, as in all medieval intellectual activity, the purpose of poetry was the same—service and preservation of the prevailing society. As the clerical writers praised their church and its beliefs, so the secular poets glorified their social class and its conventions. Unlike some modern poets the medieval poets did not attempt to modify the existing

[7] "Studien zum Formproblem des Minnesangs," *Deutsche Vierteljahrsschrift*, I (1923), 61–103.
[8] Hollander, *The Skalds*, 19.

ideals, to barter one religious, political, or social structure for another, or even, failing such massive conversion, to bring their fellow-men salvation by introducing improvements in the existing social structure; rather they attempted to retain the social structure, for it had long since discovered the way to salvation. The smallest modifications, even such that we might consider advances, were feared to undermine the whole social structure; that forests of Walther's youth had been converted into arable lands was no less a cause for sorrow than the departure from the gay courtly customs he had known (124.10, 124.18, and 124.17, 34):

bereitet ist daz velt,   verhouwen ist der walt:
   the fields are ploughed and sowed,   the forests all hewn
                                                down:

Owê wie jæmerlîche   junge liute tuont,
den ê vil hovelîchen   ir gemüete stuont!
      Alas how full of sorrow   the young folks now appear,
   who always formerly   were full of courtly cheer.

iemer mêre ouwê.
   Alas, alas, alas.

Since medieval poetry set out from accepted bases, since its purpose was to preserve the existing order, poets directed their chief efforts at presenting their material in attractive and elegant forms. Their goal, to us possibly an external one, was the employment of techniques of phrasing and the manipulation of metrical and riming possibilities for the production of a finely chiseled line or stanza.

Likewise the audiences for both Skaldic and courtly poetry were interested chiefly in the form in which a poet presented his work. Their material the medieval courtly poets took from France; we should call many of the courtly epics translations. But a poet ran the risk of being condemned as a story-spoiler if he departed from his source as was Wolfram by Gottfried, who confined himself to presenting the *Tristan*

137

story as he found it, but with all the stylistic and prosodic refinements he could muster. Northern audiences too directed their attention to construction, being quick to point out flaws in it but paying little heed to the veracity of content. When Egil finished reciting the somewhat questionable and possibly even ironic account of Eric's valiant deeds, Eric praised him, and awarded him his life for having presented his poem so well, but took no note of the content.

Verse of both types demanded highly trained audiences. Even though studies have shown that the Skaldic poems do not manipulate words with the complete abandon that was once assumed for them, an audience unused to their stylized syntax would be baffled by their word order, and possibly even fail to detect the formal requirements, such as the rimes and half-rimes mingled with alliteration, which for Skaldic poetry were supreme. The fanciers of Skaldic verse were, however, quick to detect flaws in construction, as when Harold criticized the skald Thiódólf for riming *skǫmm* with *grǫm*.[9] The pedantic devotion to detail of form among the successors of the medieval courtly poets, who maintained and were overwhelmed by the restrictions of form, is illustrated in Wagner's *Meistersinger of Nürnberg.*

Accordingly, two of the genres of Germanic verse for which we have extensive evidence were designed for limited audiences and contained limited subject matter: the courtly poetry which flourished from the last quarter of the twelfth to the end of the thirteenth century, and Skaldic poetry, which flourished from the ninth to the fourteenth. Successive generations of poets were not expected by their audiences to distinguish themselves by the introduction of new material, and as a result they turned their entire attention to the manipulation and development of external forms.

When reading the courtly poetry we find a greater and

[9] *Ibid.,* 204 ff.

greater attention to form and a progressive neglect of con-
crete detail or of any content except that required by convention. In the early minnesongs the protagonists are still human, the situation however conventionalized, as we may see
in a poem of Kürenberc, *MF* 9.21 :

Wîp vile schœne,   nu var du sam mir.
lieb unde leide   daz teile ich sant dir.
die wîle unz ich das leben hân   sô bist du mir vil liep.
wan minnest einen bœsen,   des engan ich dir niet.
    Lady very pretty,   now come thou with me.
    Joy as well as sorrow,   those will I share with thee.
    As long as I my life shall have   my love you'll never miss.
    Yet if you love a lesser,   that ne'er will I permit.

While Kürenberc presents figures, not simply emotions, while
he deals with the effects of love on a knight and a lady, neither
of them could be distinguished from any of their contemporaries. Minnesong is still young and vital enough to prevent
the poet from dealing entirely in abstractions, as does Heinrich von Morungen in the following poem, written perhaps
half a century later, *MF* 132.27 :

Ist ir liep mîn leit und ungemach,
    wie solt ich dan iemer mêre rehte werden frô?
sin getrûrte nie, swaz mir geschach:
    klagte ich ir mîn jâmer, sô stuont ir daz herze hô.
sist noch hiute vor den ougen mîn als si was dô
    dô si minneclîche mir zuo sprach
und ichs ane sach.
owê, solte ich iemer stên alsô.
    If she likes whate'er me makes unwell,
        how can I then ever more for noble pleasures try?
    She has ne'er bewailed what me befell;
        woes might I report, yet always were her spirits high.
    She's today before my eyes as then when she was nigh,
        when of love to me I heard her tell
    and my glance on her fell.
    Alas, must I always stand and sigh?

139

At this stage of minnesong the figures stand dimly behind the emotions and are quite subordinate to them; joy and sorrow are now the protagonists of the poem, involving almost secondarily the knight and his lady. The formal requirements, on the other hand, have risen; irregularity of rhythm, such as the anacrusis in line 3 of Kürenberc's stanza, is no longer permitted, but rather extreme regularity is observed, especially in the careful repetitions of matching lines, such as 1 : 3, 2 : 4.

Another half-century later, form dominated completely, and content was quite stereotyped, as in Konrad von Würzburg's tour de force in which every word rimes, Von der Hagen II.326:

Trût, brût, sich
mich an; man
hât rât dâ,
swâ dû nû bist.
Dîn schîn wît
gît muot guot
dem, swem sîn
pîn ark, stark ist.

> Dear cheer, see
> me; I my
> mind find there
> where thou now art.
> Thy nigh glance
> grants sheer cheer
> then when plight
> might long, strong smart.

and the following stanza, for which a paraphrase may perhaps be pardoned:

Sueze, bueze trûren,
sûren smerzen (herzen)
reine kleine mache;
kluogen vuogen schoene
loene mêre sêre,

niuwe riuwe swache:
lich rich lehen mir,
wîp, lîp vlehen sol wol dir.
>Dear, heal my sorrows;
>the bitter pains (in my heart)
>make very small.
>Refined and beautiful manner
>reward greatly;
>new sorrows soften:
>a rich fief give to me,
>oh lady, I earnestly pray thee.

It is hardly an unfair imputation that Konrad regarded words, not emotions whether abstract or actual, the substance of his poem. These three examples may be taken to illustrate the development of form in minnesong, as well as the changing relationships between form and content.

Kürenberc's form is not complicated, nor is it unique. His stanza consists of four lines, each divided into half-lines of three stresses, and bound by rime. At this early stage of minnesong, irregularities of rhythm are permitted which are not suggested by the content; for example, though one may assume that the first two lines of Kürenberc's poem begin with a stressed syllable unaccompanied by an unstressed to make the lines parallel and to emphasize *wîp* and *lieb,* no reason based on content or form can be suggested for the choice of anacrusis in the second half-line of two, but not in that of one. Even other asymmetries were allowed, such as the impure rime, *liep* : *niet.* Moreover, a form might be frequently repeated by the early minnesingers and borrowed by their contemporaries; Kürenberc wrote many lyrics in this form, as did his contemporaries, not least the author of the *Nibelungenlied* who throughout his epic used it modified by an additional beat in the last half-line.

At the height of minnesong, poets composed a new form for any new poem and did not repeat their forms in later poems, nor borrow forms from their contemporaries. Specific structural requirements were observed, as in the cited poem of Heinrich: the stanza is tripartite, with the first two parts identical in rhythm; the rhythm is even; the rimes, while soon to become stale by repetition, are perfect even when as here they are required four times per stanza. Yet a poet's supremacy was not tested simply by his ability to meet these requirements; more subtle manipulation of form was sought. Besides enjoying the new form and melody of this poem, Heinrich's audience must have delighted in his skillful command over his language, as shown in the line wherein Heinrich uses the monotonously repeated *e*-vowels in describing his long-drawn-out grief : *iemer mêre rehte werden . . .* , or in the antithetical *ir liep : mîn leit,* and *klagte ich ir mîn jâmer : sô stuont ir daz herze hô.* Similar control over form may be observed in the other supreme minnesingers, Reinmar and Walther von der Vogelweide, as well as a similar treatment of the conventions of love.

Later minnesingers were faced with thoroughly exploited material and thoroughly exploited forms. Their solution is illustrated in the poem of Konrad. No new content is introduced, and no new structural principles. Konrad sought eminence by applying the strict formal principles to the minutest part of his poem. Invention of new forms, turns, phrases, and rimes beyond his was hardly possible. His successors simply took over the forms of their predecessors.

No Skaldic poetry is extant that would parallel the stage of minnesong exemplified in the Kürenberc poem. Our oldest Skaldic poetry, that of Bragi, corresponds in form much more nearly to the stage of minnesong found in Heinrich von Morungen's poetry. Bragi's poems contain all the essentials of Skaldic form: restriction in the use of anacrusis and in the length of line; the involved kennings; alliteration combined with *hendings,* though these do not conform to the patterns observed in later Skaldic verse. In contrast, the poems of Kürenberc lack the most distinctive formal elements of minnesong, sharing with it only the subject matter. An earlier form of the Skaldic poems, however, can be found in the Germanic songs of praise; again content is similar, form different. Since both genres, minnesong and Skaldic poetry, offer similarities in their emphasis on form rather than matter, and in their relation to their audience, one may look for parallels in other respects, using the more completely preserved minnesong to make inferences about the origin of Skaldic verse. A more detailed discussion of this problem will be presented in the following chapter. Here we may limit ourselves to the observation that as the courtly audience of the south concentrated its attention on presentation of its ideals in ever more refined form, so the warriors of the north demanded a constantly improved form in their songs of praise. And, as in the south, attempts to refine external form were not hampered by the necessity of providing new material.

The first stanza of Bragi's *Ragnarsdrápa* may be cited as an example of the earliest Skaldic art known to us:

Vilið Hrafnketill heyra,
  hvé hreingróit steini
Þrúðar skalk ok þengil
  þjófs iljablað leyfa.
    Wilt Hrafn-ketil harken,
      how hue-bright of glow,
    Thrud's shall I and thee, prince,
      thief's sole-blade praise offer.

The form has been discussed above in Chapter 2: apart from the lack of regularly including *skothendings* in every odd line and *aðalhendings* in every even line, Bragi's verse meets all the requirements of Skaldic verse at its height, as illustrated in the following stanza from Sigvatr Þórðarson's *Bersǫglisvísur*, 3:

Gekk við móð hinn mikla,
Mǫgnús, alt í gǫgnum
ferð, þars flotnar bǫrðusk,
faðir þínn liði sínu.
Varði hart, en hjǫrtu
hugfull við þat skullu,
(Áleifr réð svá) jǫfra
erfðir (framm at hverfa).

> Stout in mind, the mighty,
> Magnus, all he staggered
> mid the fiercest warfare,
> thy father on his way.
> Battled hard; then hearts
> of heroes saw with cheer,
> (Olav resolved) foes quail
> (on, in haste to conquer).

The *aðalhendings* are perfect : *mǫg-* : *gǫg-, ín-* : *sín-, -full* : *skull-, erf-* : *hverf-;* the *skothendings* fit the requirements as well : *gekk* : *mik-, fer-* : *bǫr-, hart* : *hjǫrt-, -leifr* : *jǫfr-.* As in Konrad's verse, content hardly applies distinctively to one individual, but requirements of form are fully satisfied.

When we compare these two genres for presentation of material, we again find a similarity. Neither strives to build a structure of thought nor to develop one idea in the space of a stanza or poem. Rather, certain motifs are chosen—in Heinrich's poem, love, sorrow, misery; in Sigvatr's warfare, courage, retreat. These are fitted together, giving an effect like that one receives from many medieval church windows; one admires excellent details: in the windows a pattern of certain colors; in the Skaldic poems a pattern of *hendings;* in minnesong a pattern of rimes. But in this observation of details, the whole is often lost. Hermann Paul long ago compared minnesong with mosaics. The mosaic construction can also be observed in Skaldic poems, especially those in which the form is determined by description of a shield where the scenes are of necessity presented bit by bit as the guide points out noteworthy segments.

As a result of this type of presentation and the emphasis on poetic form, colloquial syntax patterns were neglected in Skaldic verse and in late minnesong. Konrad's highly concise syntax alone does not permit him to fulfill the requirements for his form in the second poem cited above; he finds it further necessary to introduce a parenthetical word. This is paralleled in Sigvatr's stanza and throughout Skaldic verse, though here the parenthetical element consists of a full clause. Content had long ago been subsidiary; concern with colloquial language patterns now too was coming to be secondary. Poets and audience were putting such high demands on external form that it required an artificial language as well as artificial content.

Just as minnesong and Skaldic poetry developed with their audiences, so with them they perished. The fourteenth century in Germany brought into prominence the merchant class and the decline of the courts; a small segment of the new class, striving to maintain minnesong, took a minute observance of external formal requirements to be the touchstone of true poetry. The end of the small courts in the north removed also the audience of the skalds. While the large royal court was maintained, its desire to be remembered by future generations was satisfied by the newly introduced chronicles which had the speciously enduring quality of parchment. Both genres were maintained for some time after their original audience had been removed; the forms of minnesong by the guild singers of the south; the Skaldic poems on the farms and in the church of Iceland, possibly in part through the propaganda efforts of Snorri Sturluson. With the artificial audiences the old forms became as sterile as was the joust after the invention of the crossbow. The rules of the game were known and observed rigidly by practitioners who were happy if they could fill them without content, originality, or art.

As the audience for Germanic poetry changed, so did the manner of presentation. The shift to a reading audience came earliest in the southern poetry. The poets who introduced the long epics first designed them for recitation, as for example the *Beowulf,* but their successors sought to emulate the classical authors in type of presentation as well as in dignity of form, in having their words read as well as expanded to epic proportions. Accordingly form no longer appealed to the ear alone, but also to the eye. The new awareness of this type of appeal is clear from the use of features of arrangement dependent on written letters, such as the use of acrostics. Otfrid introduces several acrostics of no mean length, the one in Preface 3 based on the dedicatory sentence: *Otfridus Uuizanburgensis Monachus Hartmuate et Uuerinberto Sancti Galli Monasterii Monachis.* "Otfrid, a monk at Weissenburg, to Hartmut and Werinbert, monks at the monastery of St. Gall." Cynewulf's self-identification by means of runes, as in the *Elene* 1269–75, is well known. We find nothing similar in the northern works of the time, even in those which were composed with great care by poets who were aware of writing symbols, such as Egil's curse consisting of the magical number of twenty-four runes employed three times per stanza. In the ninth century, therefore, many of the southern poets had not only shifted their manner of presentation, they were also aware of the increased possibilities of communication that the new presentation afforded.

The change from oral to written presentation brought also more subtle innovations into Germanic verse than external formal features like the acrostics—changes which led to a separation of units of prosody and units of meaning. In the oldest alliterative verse, one long line contained a unit of meaning, as in the Merseburg charm cited above. Moreover, while the first lift of the second half-line was the most important one for determining the alliteration of the line, the narrative material in the earliest Germanic verse composed for recitation was usually conveyed in the first half-lines; throughout the alliterating lines of this charm the second half-lines amplify or make specific the material presented in the first half-lines, but only in the last line, which is in rime, does the second half-line introduce new information, and even this merely expands the material presented in the first half-line. During the recital of the first half-line the audience would have been most receptive to new material; in the second half-line, the poet could dwell on formal and stylistic features, delighting his audience or reinforcing the meaning with a prosodic figure, or with a striking synonym or metaphor. To follow the story the members of the audience could let their attention lag when the second half-lines were recited, as in the following stanza from the *Song of Weland* 30:

Úti stendr kunnig   kván Níðaðar,
ok hon inn um gekk   endlangan sal.
En hann á salgarð   settiz at hvílaz—:
"Vakir þú, Níðuðr,   Niára dróttinn?"
    Without stands the wily   wife of Níðuð,
    and she went inside   throughout the hall;
    but he on the hall-fence   holds his rest:
    "Are you awake, Níðuð,   the Niarar's king?"

In line 1 of this stanza the material of the second half-line merely completes that of the first half-line, though it is not completely appositional as is the material of the second half-line of line 4. In line 2 *endlangan sal* makes graphic the content of the adverbs *inn* and *um*. Only the second half-line of line 3 continues the narrative material of the first half-line.

Other Germanic poetry designed for recitation may not concentrate so markedly the narrative material in the first half-line, but, as may be observed in reading the Old Norse and early Old English poetry, conforms to the examples cited in making the long line a unit of sense and in bringing little new material in the second half-line, especially at its end. Detailed comment would extend this discussion unduly; further examples illustrating this allotment of functions may be found in the material cited earlier, as in the stanzas from the *Song of Weland* cited above in Chapter 2. On first analysis this observation does not seem to be borne out in some second half-lines, for example, *Song of Weland* 31.1 : *Vaki ek ávalt, vilia lauss.* *Vilia lauss* seems designed to introduce new narrative material; but its primary importance is stylistic, for it repeats a phrase used earlier of Weland after Niðuð had taken him captive and had inaugurated the action that led to Weland's revenge:

Sat hann svá lengi,   at hann sofnaði,
       ok hann vaknaði   vilia lauss:

Lines 31.2 and 4 continue the narrative material throughout the line, to be sure, but the ten other second half-lines of this passage have essentially a stylistic and metrical function. The recited Germanic long line accordingly divided the two prime functions among its half-lines: the second contained the most important metrical and stylistic material, the first the most important narrative material.

When poems were designed to be read, whether silently or aloud, the audience might be as alert, or drowsy, over the first half-line as over the second. Accordingly the advantages of presenting new material in the first half-line were lost. Especially in the new book epic, patterned on Roman writers, the old distribution of material was abandoned. Poems consisting of thousands of lines, rather than a hundred or two, would have seemed extremely monotonous if each line were a sense unit as well as a metrical unit. Such monotony was avoided through the expedient of carrying on sense units over an ex-

148

tent of metrical units. Furthermore, poets soon hit on the device of crossing sense and metrical units, of breaking their sense units at the middle of metrical units. Composition for a reading audience therefore provided two reasons for the change in emphasis on the half-lines : the desire for epic continuity, and the lack of control over the alertness of the audience. Both contributed to transfer the narrative function to the second half-line, leaving the first half-line free for the characteristic stylistic pattern of the south, a variation which was pointed out in a review by J. Franck.[10] In contrast with the northern Eddic verse, the sense of book epics may often be derived from the second half-lines alone, as in the *Heliand* 249 ff. :

> Thô uuarð is uuîsbodo
> an Galilealand, Gabriel cuman,
> engil thes alouualdon, thar he êne idis uuisse,
> munilîca magað : Maria uuas sie hêten,
> uuas iru thiorna githigin. Sea ên thegan habda,
> Ioseph gimahlit, gôdes cunnies man,
> thes Dauides dohter : that uuas sô diurlîc uuîf,
> idis anthêti.

> Then was his messenger
> to Galilee, Gabriel come,
> angel of the Lord, where a lady he knew,
> a dear maiden Mary was she called,
> she was a grown maiden. She had married a thane,
> to Joseph she was given, a man of good descent,
> the daughter of David ; a very dear woman was she,
> a pious lady.

In this passage new narrative material is given only in two of the seven first half-lines, in 254a (line 6 above), and possibly in 250a (line 2 above), though here the narrative function of the name is hardly more important than the stylistic. Although this passage is almost extreme, a similar concentra-

[10] *AfdA*, 37 (1917), 6–14.

149

tion of narrative material in the second half-lines is not at all unusual in the West Germanic book epics. We may assume that the change from an audience of listeners to one of readers had brought about a complete reversal in the use of the individual half-lines: material introduced for rhetorical and stylistic effect was now presented in the first half-lines, and meaning units accordingly were stretched beyond metrical units.

This new arrangement we find in subsequent poetry belonging to the same tradition, when poets were not unduly hampered by lack of control over form. Even in the earliest Old English poetry the first half-line is often filled with rhetorical material, as in some lines of the *Fight at Finnsburg* noted above; in later Old English poetry the distribution of function in the two half-lines is similar to that illustrated in the *Heliand* lines, e.g., *Judith*, 141 ff.:

<pre>
                    Wiggend sǣton,
weras wæccende   wearde hēoldon
in ðām fæstenne,   swa ðām folce ǣr
gēomormōdum   Iudith bebēad,
searoðoncol mægð,   þā hēo on sīð gewāt,
idis ellenrōf.
</pre>

<pre>
                    The warriors were sitting,
    the men waking,   their watch holding,
    in the fastness,   where the folk earlier,
    those bereft of joy,   Judith had ordered,
    the wise maiden,   when she went on her trip,
    the valiant woman.
</pre>

Again the first half-lines supplement the second half-lines.

When rime is introduced into epic poetry the long line is no longer a unit; accordingly the meaning is more equably distributed and narrative material is equally apportioned among odd and even lines, as in the following passage from Otfrid, 2.14.13:

Unz drúhtin thar saz éino,   so quam ein wíb thara thó,
tház si thes gizíloti,   thes wázares gihóloti.
    Our Lord sat there alone,   then came a woman thereto,
    who had that as her aim,   that after water she there came.

We may note, however, that when poetry is again designed
for recitation, the function of half-lines resembles that of the
half-lines of Germanic alliterative poetry in verse written in
long lines with a distinct caesura, for example, in the Middle
High German *Nibelungenlied,* 4:

Ir pflâgen drîe künege   edel unde rîch,
Gunther unde Gernôt,   di recken lobelîch,
und Gîselher der junge,   ein ûz erwelter degen.
diu frouwe was ir swester,   die fürsten hetens in ir pflegen.
    Three kings took care of her   noble and strong,
    Gunther and Gernot,   the heroes famed in song,
    and Giselher the young,   a knight without compare.
    The lady was their sister,   the princes had her in their
                          care.

As in the early Germanic poetry the second half-lines consist
of explanatory material, supplementing the narrative presented in the first half-lines. The *Nibelungenlied,* designed for
recitation like the Germanic epics, again exhibits characteristics of external form which resulted from the manner of
presentation.

From the twelfth century on, courtly lyric poetry was
designed for singing, not recitation. This type of presentation
invaded Germany and England with the conventions of
courtly love. To be sure, lyric poetry for singing had existed
previously, though melodies were relatively simple, possibly
somewhat like those of the older Faroese and Norwegian song
dances. A contemporary, Giraldus Cambrensis, notes a distinct difference between the song of south and north England
and ascribes it to the Scandinavian influence in the north.[11]

[11] See Josef M. Müller-Blattau, "Musikalische Studien zur altgermanischen Dichtung," *Deutsche Vierteljahrsschrift,* 3 (1925), 536–65.

In the earlier lyric, lines written in ostensibly the same form could vary in the location of stress, in type of rhythm, and in the number of syllables, as do lines of the Kürenberc poem quoted above, *MF* 9.21. In the first line, *wîp vile schœne,* two stresses stand side by side on *wîp* and *vil-;* in the next two lines the rhythm is trochaic, in the fourth iambic; the fifth, *die wîle unz ich das leben hân,* has trisyllabic anacrusis. Other poems of Kürenberc have a completely different rhythm, though in the same form, e.g., *MF* 9.14:

Es gât mir vonme herzen   daz ich geweine:
ich und mîn geselle   müezen uns scheiden. . . .
    It touches all my heart,   so that I am weeping:
    I from my companion   must now be leaving. . . .

When one reads Kürenberc one observes clearly that he and the other early minnesingers had not advanced far beyond the tendency to even rhythm that can be observed in the Old High German poets.

In the courtly lyric proper, accompanying melodies were composed in a measured form of music that had become widespread in the eleventh century, the so-called *descant.* Verse written to the accompaniment of such melodies did not permit the variation in rhythm from line to line and stanza to stanza that we find in Kürenberc. Possibly the regularity was brought about by the innovation of descant, that unlike the earlier music it provided a definite measure for song. Measures of the first two modes could consist of a long note having the value of three or be divided into two unequal sections, one with a value of two, the other with a value of one. It is customary to distinguish three prime modes, with the following rhythms:

First: ♩♪ | ♩♪ |
Second: ♪♩ | ♪♩ |
Third: ♩♪♪ | ♩♪♪ |

Romance verse written in lines consisting of fewer than ten syllables were set to melodies in one of the first two modes, those of more than ten, often in the third mode. Lines of five syllables then might be written to a melody with a rhythm

$\acute{-} \smile \mid \acute{-} \smile \mid \acute{-}$ or $\smile - \mid \smile - \mid \smile .$

At the Festival of Mainz in 1184 the German lyric poets came to know such melodies and poems set to them. The conventions of courtly love had invaded Germany from the Provence a few decades earlier, but the old popular song forms had not been displaced immediately among the courtly poets; the earliest poems that had adopted the courtly motif of considering the woman rather than the man the object of affection are still in the old form. At the Festival of Mainz, to which Frederick Barbarossa invited nobles from Romance as well as Germanic areas, German poets came into personal contact with French and Provençal poets. Though we have no records of the poets present at the Festival, we can make inferences about individual poets. One of the French nobles present was the patron of the poet Guiot of Provins; from his presence we can assume that Guiot himself was there. A contemporary German poet who was almost certainly present was the widely traveled Friderich von Husen. After the time of the Festival, German poets began to compose lyrics on the French pattern.

Presumably the first German poem in the new form is Friderich von Husen's *Ich denke under wîlen*. We make this assumption because it broke with German tradition in introducing three rimes in the stollen. *Ich denke under wîlen* was written to a melody of Guiot's,[12] and it follows Guiot's arrangement of rime, anacruses, and cadences, though it does not translate the French words. Since this poem so clearly

---

[12] This is given in modern notation in Carl von Kraus, *Des Minnesangs Frühling, Untersuchungen* (Leipzig, 1939), 126–27.

brought Romance form to minnesong, from a comparison of it with an earlier German lyric, we may observe the changes which were introduced into the form of German minnesong from Romance poetry.

We must note first, however, that the introduction of the tripartite form alone would not have evened out the rhythm, nor would a syllable-by-syllable imitation of Romance verse. For Romance verse rhythm was based on the number of syllables per line, German verse rhythm on the number of stresses. The two rhythms are quite remote from each other until one compares the musical form; melodies in descant were adaptable to poetry with a fixed number of syllables, whether the selection of these was based primarily on their number, like the Romance, or on their accent, like the German. When now the German poets adopted some of the French melodies, and more important, when they adopted the practice of composing melodies to their lyrics in descant, the new type of presentation sharply circumscribed their form.

To illustrate the effect we may compare with *Ich denke under wîlen* a poem which von Kraus, *MFU* 82, calls the most beautiful of the early minnesongs (*MF* 37.4):

Ez stuont ein frouwe alleine
und warte uber heide
und warte ire liebe,
so gesach si valken fliegen.
"sô wol dir, valke, daz du bist!
du fliugest swar dir liep ist:
du erkiusest dir in dem walde
einen boum der dir gevalle.
alsô hân ouch ich getân:
ich erkôs mir selbe einen man,
den erwelten mîniu ougen,
daz nîdent schœne frouwen.
owê wan lânt si mir mîn liep?
jô 'ngerte ich ir dekeiner trûtes niet."

154

A lady stood alone
and looked over the plain
and looked for her lover;
then she saw a falcon hover.
"Hail to you, falcon, there on high,
wheree'er it pleases you you fly:
in the forest for yourself you choose
any tree that may you please.
Just so have I also done.
I chose for myself a man,
whom my own eyes elected;
then lovely women me suspected.
Why don't they let me have my love?
Their favorites I ne'er did them begrudge."

The first stanza of *Ich denke under wîlen* goes as follows:

Ich denke under wîlen,
ob ich ir nâher wære,
waz ich ir wolte sagen.
daz kürzet mir die mîlen,
swenn ich ir mîne swære
sô mit gedanken klage.
mich sehent mange tage
diu liute in der gebære
als ich niht sorgen habe,
wan ichs alsô vertrage.

> I think from while to while,
> if to her I might go,
> what I to her would say.
> That shortens many a mile,
> when I to her my woe
> thus in my mind betray.
> The world many a day
> sees me behaving so,
> as I had no complaint,
> for I'll not it display.

When we compare the two poems we note little improvement
in purity of rime. Though a greater proportion of his rimes

155

are pure, Friderich avoided assonance no more than did the author of the earlier poem. The great difference, however, is to be found in the structure of the stanza and in its rhythm.

In Friderich's poem the form is clearly articulated; the divisions into stollen and *abgesang* are immediately obvious. In the early poem, on the other hand, the structure is so veiled that there has been considerable dispute about the length of the stollen and *abgesang,* and even some question whether the stanza is written in tripartite form. We may follow Von Kraus's analysis into two stollen of four lines, and an *abgesang* of six, since it is supported by arrangement of content as well as form. Far from being confronted with such difficulties of analysis in minnesong after Von Husen, we find the tripartite division one of the most apparent external formal features.

But while the new melodies brought about such clear articulation of subdivisions, their greatest effect was on the rhythm. After the introduction of Romance melody, the practice of permitting two contiguous accented syllables, as in 37.9 *liep ist,* was abandoned. Similarly two successive unaccented syllables, as in 37.10 *erkiusest dir in dem walde,* was no longer permitted, unless one of the syllables in question could be elided or was very light. Nor was anacrusis varied at will. A structure was determined for one line of a stanza, and repeated exactly in the corresponding line of matching stollen or stanzas. Similarly, when more than one stanza was composed in one poem, that is, to one melody, the structure and rhythm was maintained without change as may be observed in the remaining stanzas of *Ich denke under wîlen,* and in the *minnelieder* of Walther and his contemporaries.

Accordingly, though linguistic changes had evened out many of the irregularities of the Germanic line, the perfection of form that we admire in minnesong at its height was accomplished only after the combination of Germanic verse with Romance song. The new presentation brought symmetry

in any selected form, but still permitted the poet initial freedom in evolving the form he considered appropriate for any
given poem. Elements he could vary at will from poem to
poem were his rime scheme, anacrusis, length, and cadence of
each line, as well as length of stollen and *abgesang;* accordingly he was given great freedom in the form of his lines and
stanzas but had to adhere to any pattern that was once
chosen.

The aim for perfection in form constantly grew stronger
in minnesong. Shortly after Von Husen's poem was composed, irregularities maintained in it, such as impure rimes,
were no longer tolerated. Compare any of Walther's poems,
for example the one cited above (p. 60). We have already
noted the culmination of this trend to the elaborate forms of
the late minnesingers, and also the inability of Konrad's successors to devise new forms to fit such existing standards.
They accordingly used and re-used forms of the minnesingers,
producing the sterility of meistersong.

In England the great period of Romance influence came
later than the time of courtly poetry. A few French lyrics in
the courtly tradition have come down to us from England;
their authors may have exerted an influence on poets composing in English, for lyrics written about 1300 show the striving for perfection of form and tripartite division, as in the
following stanza:

Lenten yz come wiþ loue to toune,   (*Lenten,* 'spring'; *to toune,*
                                          'to stay')
Wiþ blosmen & wiþ briddes roune,

  Þat al þis blisse bryngeþ;

Dayes-eʒes in þis dales,   (*Dayes-eʒes,* 'daisies')

Notes suete of nyhtegales,

157

Vch foul song singeþ.

Þe þrestelcoc him þreteþ oo,	('The thrush is always exciting them')
Away is huere wynter wo,	(*huere,* 'their')
When woderoue springeþ;	(*woderoue,* 'woodruff')
Þis foules singeþ ferly fele,	(*ferly fele,* 'marvelously many')
Ant wlyteþ on huere wynter wele,	(*wlyteþ,* 'warble'; *wele,* 'joy')
Þat al þe wode ryngeþ.	

Yet it remained for Chaucer and his contemporaries to adopt Romance verse form as completely as did the minnesingers, and to produce poetry which might equal theirs.

In the north too the Romance influence brought a completely regular rhythm only after the thirteenth century, but again verse of no high order, as may be noted from the example cited above (p. 47).

When we study the changes of Germanic verse form in relation to changes of audience and presentation, we note a correlation as we had between changes in verse and linguistic form. As new audiences arise, the old verse forms are modified; as new types of presentation are favored, different roles are assigned to segments of form and previous formal requirements are altered.

In general, the effects upon form of presentation and audience are secondary to those of language, or they affect larger segments of form. When minnesong was written to the accompaniment of a strict musical form, lines were completely evened and made parallel in rhythm. The new type of presentation accordingly completed a trend in verse form that had been initiated several centuries earlier by linguistic changes. When epics were produced for a reading audience, grosser formal elements like acrostics were introduced, and the function of sections in the line altered. The first half-line, which in recited poetry contained the essential narrative material, now was employed for the introduction of ornamentation, and narrative material was presented in the second half-line.

Similarly, as audiences grow more select, they place greater formal demands on poets rather than initiate formal innovations. The skalds and minnesingers were compelled to devote more and more of their attention to the refinements of form, and eventually these became so complex that content and normal language patterns came to be secondary. The late skalds and minnesingers fulfilled all the formal requirements of their genres, but at the expense of new content and normal syntax.

Possibly the most conclusive demonstration of the relationship of forms and audience may be found in the fate of Skaldic poetry and minnesong. When social changes removed their audiences, these two genres were abandoned or artificially maintained. The conventions of love that minnesong proclaimed still form the basis of the modern attitude on love in Western civilization; the forms in which minnesong proclaimed these conventions, however, except for their continued maintenance among the hapless meistersinger, perished in the thirteenth century.

5 CHANGE IN DIRECTION OF INFLUENCE AND VERSE FORM

While linguistic changes were gradually modifying the structure of the Germanic languages, the native poets were being exposed to new literary traditions and theory as they turned from their former beliefs to Christianity. The church brought with it the classical Latin authors—Vergil, Ovid, Statius—and their Christian successors—Prudentius, Arator, and the hymn writers. Since its cultural centers introduced and maintained the same traditions in Germanic as in Romance areas, the Germanic cultural leaders became thoroughly acquainted with the Latin literature relatively early. Poems in Latin and in the Latin literary tradition were being composed in Germanic areas earlier than any of the Germanic literary works which have come down to us. Shortly after the time that the oldest Germanic poem hitherto discovered was being scratched on the Eggjum stone in Norway, approximately A.D. 650, Bede in England was writing not only accomplished Latin hymns but also a treatise on meter. Several centuries later two students of Hrabanus Maurus produced the most eminent poetry of their age in Germany, Walafrid Strabo in Latin, Otfrid in Old High German; again the German poem can hardly have been undertaken before Walafrid died in 849. Accordingly it is almost inconceivable that any of the Germanic poets, except perhaps the early Scandinavians, can have been unaware of the Latin poetic tradition, whether this was transmitted to them indirectly through Romance areas, by Celts, or directly through the church.

The turn towards the south set the direction of literary influence for centuries. When it began is uncertain. That the plastic arts were affected by it before the time of Bede is clear from the objects found recently in the burial mound at Sutton Hoo which were fashioned before 650. Yet the plastic arts probably lend themselves to imitation much more readily than do literary works. Monasteries were required for the Latin poetic tradition to become thoroughly installed. In England these were established in the early part of the seventh century, in Germany in the latter part of the eighth. All our poetry from England and Germany, even the secular, was very likely composed in monasteries or by men trained in them. Certainly the literary remains were transmitted through them, even the scraps of popular superstition such as the charms. It remains to ask what were the influences exerted on Germanic form by the Latin and Romance traditions which were paramount in these monasteries.

When the two literary traditions met, they brought together a number of differing elements of form. Latin poetry was written in regular rhythms, often specific meters, while the rhythm of Germanic poetry was quite irregular. A great portion of the Latin poetry was bound with end rime. Latin forms existed in greater variety and greater extent than the Germanic. These differences did not escape Bede, and they can hardly have escaped later Germanic poets. For the Germanic monks not only read and heard Latin poetry, they also practiced it. The monasteries must have contained poets writing for two different audiences: those like Bede and Strabo, who were writing for the Latin audience, and those like Caedmon and Otfrid, who were writing for the Germanic. In such a setting it is surprising that the two separate literary traditions maintained their identity to the extent that they did.

161

Irish native tradition, by contrast, was overwhelmed by the Latin. The native free alliterative verse was abandoned in favor of a syllable-counting rimed verse that merely maintained for ornament the characteristic structural features of the older poetry, such as alliteration. Moreover, this very feature was incorporated for ornament into the Latin verse of the Irish poets. After the Latin and the native Irish traditions had met, rime and a fixed number of syllables regulated the form of Irish poetry, but alliteration was maintained in great measure as adornment. In the Germanic area neither literary stream abandoned itself to the other so completely. Here the mutual influences exert themselves much more gradually, and are much more difficult to detect than in the Celtic area. It even seems paradoxical that England, where the influence of the monasteries was established relatively early and firmly, should have maintained the Germanic alliterative form long after it was abandoned on the continent. In Germany the alliterative form was given up less than a century after the first monasteries were established, after only one attempt to compose a Christian epic in it, the *Heliand.* Even shorter poems in characteristic Germanic forms such as the song of praise, for example, the Old High German *Ludwigslied,* abandoned the native form. The solution of the paradox lies possibly in the basic reason for the maintenance, or abandonment, of Germanic poetic forms, that is, the changing linguistic structure. To this we may ascribe all of the fundamental changes of poetic form in the early Germanic languages. In Old English, linguistic changes had not yet removed the natural bases of the alliterative form. On the other hand, when poets were setting out to write Old Saxon and Old High German verse, these languages, as was shown in Chapter 3, had lost the linguistic characteristics requisite for alliterative verse.

While linguistic changes modified the smaller segments of Germanic verse form, larger formal elements were modified by the influence of foreign traditions. External influences are particularly prominent in two separate periods. In the eighth and ninth centuries the epic form was imported from Latin and Romance tradition, first in England, subsequently in Germany. In the twelfth century, Romance forms were again imported, now especially in lyric, but also in epic, poetry, and now most prominently on the continent. Other borrowings of external form have been suggested, but without conclusive evidence. Most disputed of these is Skaldic verse form, which has been ascribed to borrowing from Irish. Direct evidence for or against this view is indecisive. Since the evidence presented rests in large measure on methodology, this problem will be discussed after we have noted the results of the two periods of importation that are well established.

The importation of the epic entailed expansion of previously existing story without the introduction of any distinct structural characteristic. Story no more complex than that found in many Germanic epic songs is expanded in length and breadth through the addition of setting and tribal background, and through accounts of the hero's words and motives as well as his acts. We may compare Beowulf's encounter with three monsters or the Old English account of Moses' exploit in leading the Children of Israel out of Egypt with Weland's marriage, captivity, and revenge. In the *Beowulf* the haunts of Grendel and the halls of Heorot are minutely described; in the *Song of Weland* the scene of Weland's hunting and the halls of Niðuð are merely presented as existing. Nor do we learn about Niðuð's kingdom, or his ancestors, not to speak of the background of the supernatural Weland, whereas in the *Beowulf* the royal house of Heorot is put in a historical setting, and the mythical hero himself is identified with the ruling family of the Geats. Moreover, Beowulf is given free play to tell of his youthful heroic feats and of his decision to aid the oppressed Danes, while we ourselves have to supply the

163

motivation for Weland's mode of revenge on Bǫðvild which the unknown poet simply suggests in a most tenuous fashion by having Niðuð present her with the ring that Weland had reserved for his former wife. The *Weland* story has fully the epic possibilities of the *Beowulf*. Formal elements that distinguish the two were adopted from poetry brought to England by the monastic culture.

Only such larger elements of form differentiate the first Germanic epics from their shorter predecessors; the Germanic principles of alliteration and rhythm were maintained in the Old English and Old Saxon epics. After the twelfth century, rime replaced alliteration in the main tradition of English literature, and in Bede's terms, meter replaced rhythm. Rime and meter had been introduced by Otfrid into Old High German literature in the second half of the ninth century. The importation of the Romance lyric involved a distinct structural feature, the tripartite stanza form, which required that the lyric stanza be composed of three parts, two stollen alike in form and an *abgesang*. In this chapter the effects of importation on Germanic verse form will be studied, and their relationships to the influences that have already been discussed.

The course of development of the long epic in Old English remains obscure in its details because we do not know which is the oldest Old English epic, or even whether the religious epics like the *Genesis* preceded the epic with a secular theme, the *Beowulf*. Early scholars, still under the spell of romantic notions, assumed without question that the Germanic epic, of which only the *Beowulf* was thought to have survived, unfolded from the earlier heroic songs, and that this form was subsequently adopted by monks to aid in their proselytizing efforts. Later scholars, notably Ker, completely demolished this view of the self-growth of the Germanic epic. Furthermore, the date of composition of the *Beowulf* has been steadily advanced until it is now placed as late as 750. With regard to the primacy of the secular or religious epic, there is much to be said for Marquardt's view[1] that the Old English religious epics were composed earlier, and that the *Beowulf* must be dated after some of our extant epics, such as the *Genesis* and *Exodus*. For this view does not run counter to our only early report—Bede's account of Caedmon. Moreover, it offers positive evidence based on *Beowulf* 1410:

enge ānpaðas,   uncūð gelād,
    narrow by-paths,   little-known courses,

a line which is also found in *Exodus* 58. In general, the *Exodus* poet was much more independent and much less ready to borrow than was the *Beowulf* poet. Furthermore, it is much more likely that the *Beowulf* poet lifted the line from the *Exodus*. This conclusion requires that the *Exodus,* and the *Genesis* in part, antedate the *Beowulf,* and presumably that they themselves were antedated by Caedmon's *Hymn,* though they may not have been written by Caedmon.[2] It is further plausible to assume that the long epic, imported as it must have been by the monasteries, was introduced into Germanic for religious, not secular, writings.

Stylistically few innovations were required to shift from the Germanic heroic songs and songs of praise to the Christian poems. God and Christian heroes were given epithets previously applied to earthly princes, or modified forms of these that hardly change the rhythm of the half-line. The *ēce dryhten* 'eternal Lord' of Caedmon's *Hymn* maintains precisely the rhythm of the secular *lēofne dryhten* 'dear lord'. Other epithets required only slight modification, such as *rīces weard* to *heofonrīces weard,* 'warder of the kingdom' to 'warder of the heavenly kingdom'. Although no song of praise has

---

[1] H. Marquardt, "Zur Entstehung des Beowulf," *Anglia,* 64 (1940), 152–58.

[2] Fr. Klaeber, "Noch einmal Exodus 56–58 und Beowulf 1408–10," *Archiv,* 187 (1950), 71-72, maintains, however, the opposite view.

come down to us from England, it is scarcely likely that they were absent only in this section of the Germanic world; Caedmon, or whoever the first Old English religious poet may have been, needed do little more than substitute the name of God, or Moses, for that of a secular hero to modify a pagan to a Christian poem.

We may cite passages from the *Beowulf* to illustrate how epic techniques were taken over, and further passages from the *Heliand* to illustrate how they were maintained in subsequent religious epics. A few lines from the description of Grendel's abode may demonstrate the new fondness for describing the setting. While the shorter lays are content to state the facts of a hero's battle and victory, the *Beowulf* depicts in great detail the scene of Beowulf's triumph, 1357 ff.:

> Hīe dȳgel lond
> warigeað wulfhleoþu,   windige næssas,
> frēcne fengelād,   ðǣr fyrgenstrēam
> under næssa genipu   niþer gewīteð,
> flōd under foldan.   Nis þæt feor heonon
> mīlgemearces,   þæt se mere standeð;
> ofer þǣm hongiað   hrinde bearwas,
> wudu wyrtum fæst   wæter oferhelmað.
>
> They unknown land
> possess, wolf-cliffs,   windy nesses,
> dangerous fen-paths   where fell streams
> under the nesses' darkness   downward fall,
> flood under the earth.   Not farther hence is that
> than a mile's distance,   where the mere is;
> round over it hang   rime-covered groves,
> a wood fast-rooted   the water overshadows.

And almost as if to point out the source of his innovation the poet a few lines later includes in his description line 1410 cited above which corresponds remarkably to *Aeneid* 9.525:

angustaeque ferunt faucēs aditūsque malīgnī
    Narrow defiles bore them on their way and evil courses . . .

Similarly the author of the Old Saxon *Heliand* provides his audience with the setting for one of the deeds of his hero which must have impressed his North German audience greatly, the calming of the waves, 2241 ff.:

> Thuo bigan thes uuedares craft,
> ûst up stîgan,   ûðiun uuahsan;
> suang gisuerc an gimang;   thie sêu uuarð an hruoru,
> uuan uuind endi uuater;

> Then began the strength of the wind,
> the storm to roar,   the waves to rise;
> darkness descended;   the sea rose to an uproar,
> fought wind with water.

Such descriptions one seeks in vain in the Skaldic poems or in the Old High German *Ludwigslied;* Ludwig encountered the Normans, entered battle praising God, and proceeded to perform his deed of valor. The *Beowulf* poet, on the other hand, presenting a setting very like Vergil's description of the approach to the underworld in the *Aeneid* 6.131 ff. and 237 ff., does not limit himself to an account of Beowulf's deed of valor, but has learned from Vergil how to prepare for a given epic exploit by placing it in suitable surroundings.

New also is the introduction of the historical background. Without this the feeble story of the *Beowulf*—the powerful hero dispatches several monsters through the great strength of his arm—might have made up the subject of a song of praise, certainly not a heroic ode as beautifully rounded as the *Song of Weland.* But as the Old English poet develops the poem, Beowulf's dispatching of monsters is merely an illustrious series of episodes in the early history of the Germanic peoples, especially the Danes in their relations with the Bards, Swedes, and Geats, and even with the Franks and the far-off Goths. In tales narrated at the court ceremonies and entertainments, the *Beowulf* author has succeeded in presenting the previous and present history of the various tribes

167

mentioned, putting Beowulf's slaying of the monsters into the larger background of the achievement of harmony between the Geats and the Danes. Similarly the author of the *Heliand* relates the hero to the earlier history of his people by juxtaposing the career of Jesus and John, even to the extent of rearranging his venerated sources, and by pointing up the greater significance of the Saviour, as does also Otfrid. While still pre-eminently a religious hero, Jesus in the *Heliand* is depicted as no less a national figure than is Aeneas in the *Aeneid,* or Beowulf, the folklore hero, has become in the Old English poem.

Another epic feature that was not neglected by the Germanic poets was the fondness of the epic hero for speaking, for relating his previous exploits. The older Germanic poems made great use of dialogue, but for the purpose of bearing the action, not expanding it. The exchange between Hildebrand and Hadubrand in the Old High German *Hildebrandslied* indicates the inevitability of their combat; the exchange between Unferth and Beowulf, *Beowulf* 506 ff., glorifies the hero through the introduction of his youthful swimming exploit and through comparison of his valor with the helplessness of Unferth and his companions before Grendel. The Beowulf-Unferth exchange recalls that between Odysseus and Euryalus in Phaeacia. Both foreshadow the success of the hero in the coming test; after hearing Beowulf's yarns we have small doubt about the outcome of his future struggle with Grendel. But apart from expanding the stature of the hero they have no relation to the action. In the *Heliand,* with its totally different conception of the heroic, the hero again has ample opportunity to set forth his views; the Sermon on the Mount alone makes up a disproportionate tenth of the poem.

These borrowings from the Latin epics, the expansion of the background, of the historical setting, and the hero's personality, illustrate that the earliest Germanic contact with

Latin poetry affected only the larger elements of form. Lesser features of the Graeco-Roman epic technique, such as the *epitheton ornans,* were passed over by the early English poets and their successors.

The same principle of adaptation applies to external form. Again the importation affects large segments. External form as a whole is extended; the poetic line left unmodified by foreign contact. Sections in the epics such as the *Finnsburg* tale in the *Beowulf* or the calming of the waves episode in the *Heliand* differ little from the native short, independent lays. Innovations affecting smaller elements of verse form, such as those modifying the Germanic line, were undertaken only later in southern Germany, and the new line modeled on the Romance line. But as we have noted above, the abandonment of the Germanic irregular rhythm in favor of a more even rhythm was a direct result of linguistic changes, not of borrowing. Besides leading to an even rhythm, linguistic change had reduced the primary stresses on the initial syllables of certain word-classes, especially the substantives, and had led to clausal-stress patterns in which final elements of a sentence as well as initial might be prominent. Accordingly, the new rhythm must have suggested the advantage of end rime over alliteration. When story without strong central unity, such as the life of Christ, was made the subject of the epic, the advantage of a formal element which would introduce continuity through external form must have been even more apparent. Although end rime and even rhythm were modeled after Romance verse, their way had been prepared by changes that had taken place earlier inside the Germanic languages.

A continuous tradition between the Old English epics and the first Old High German epic in the new form can hardly be doubted, though we have no explicit evidence that Otfrid knew the Old English epics. For the Old Saxon epics are closely related to the Old English, as the translation of

169

sections of the Old Saxon *Genesis* into Old English indicates. And the Old Saxon *Heliand* was probably composed in the monastery at Fulda at a time when Otfrid was a student there. While a full study of common elements of the *Heliand* and *Krist* remains to be done, Schröder has pointed out a few coincidences of detail.[3] In the earliest part of his work Otfrid referred to Mary as an *itis*, a word found elsewhere in Old High German only in the first Merseburg charm, but common in the *Heliand*. Likewise the disciples are called thanes in both epics, in the other Old High German writings, however, by the term that was to become standard in German, *Jünger*. Accordingly Schröder argues that the younger poet may have met the *Heliand* author, or even that he may have heard him read sections of his poem; and W. Foerste finds even more evidence that Otfrid knew the *Heliand*.[4] The correspondences between Otfrid's *Krist* and the *Heliand*, even without Schröder's suggestion of personal acquaintance between the Old Saxon and Old High German authors, requires us to assume a continuity of tradition from Caedmon to Otfrid.

Whether or not Otfrid knew any epics besides the *Heliand* in the Old English and Old Saxon tradition, he certainly was acquainted with the alliterative form. For the first part of his poem abounds with alliterative lines, not only the much cited line (1.18.9)

Thar ist líb ana tód, líoht ana fínstri,
  There is life without death, light without darkness,

but also many that rime as well as alliterate (1.3.37)

Iro dágo ward giwágo fon alten wízagon,
  Their days were foretold by prophets of old,

---

[3] *Forschungen und Fortschritte*, 7 (1931), 395–97.

[4] "Otfrids literarisches Verhältnis zum Heliand," *Jahrbuch des Vereins für niederdeutsche Sprachforschung*, 71–73 (Neumünster, 1950), 40–67.

and others that lack rime, though without achieving alliteration throughout (1.6.9).

Wio wárd ih io so wírdig   fora drúhtine
  How became I ever so worthy   before the Lord

Consequently we may assume that the alliterative form was available to Otfrid, and that he deliberately rejected it, probably warned by the failure of such Old High German examples as the *Muspilli*.

In his preface to Archbishop Liutbert, which deals with questions of meter and orthography and with his reasons for adopting the new form, Otfrid tells us that he chose to write in German rather than in Latin for patriotic reasons; possibly, as Schröder suggests, he did not want his own people to fall behind the Slavs who were creating a stir in the third quarter of the ninth century with their Bible translation. Prose, however, does not fulfill Otfrid's requirements; the words and deeds of Christ must be ornamented suitably (*decenter*) in his own tongue. As models for the form of his poetic work he had before him Juvencus, Arator, and Prudentius. In Prudentius he found rimed couplets in a meter consisting of four beats to the line, and in end rime. Since he was apparently aware of the shortcomings of his language in fulfilling the requirement of Germanic verse rhythm and alliteration, Otfrid chose meter and rime as binding elements for his work.

Long before Otfrid, Bede had stated the essential rhythmic difference between Latin and Germanic verse. In a passage on rhythm he says: "But it will be observed that rhythm is similar to meters, for it is a modulated arrangement of words examined by the judgment of the ear not according to metrical principles but according to the number of syllables, as in the poems of the poets writing in the vernaculars. And although rhythm can exist without meter, meter without

171

rhythm is impossible. . . ."[5] Bede accordingly considered the arrangement of words in Germanic verse to be relatively free; that in Latin poetry to be governed by metrical standards. While the free arrangement did not lack rhythm, the regulated lines of Latin verse had a further excellence in their meter. Otfrid set out to remove the difference between Latin and Germanic verse, to introduce meter into his poem.

The careful manuscripts of his poem, one of which he himself presumably corrected, illustrate nicely in one line how he set about replacing "rhythm" with "meter." In the manuscript which Otfrid is thought to have corrected, the first part of line 1.18.10 is corrected from *éngilo kúnni* to *éngilichaz kúnni;* the revision at least suggests the trochaic meter, while the earlier phrase maintains the abrupt rhythm of the alliterative verse. By modifying a few syllables, by using an adjectival rather than a nominal construction, Otfrid made the shift to meter.

The line also illustrates the very slight difference between Otfrid's "meter" and the "rhythm" of his immediate predecessors, as does even more clearly the fact that Otfrid could maintain in his poem a line occurring also in the alliterative *Muspilli*—the line immediately preceding the corrected line 1.18.9:

Thar ist líb ana tód,   líoht ana fínstri.

While ostensibly adopting the meter of his Latin models who accompanied unstressed with stressed syllables, Otfrid preserved the Germanic freedom of omitting unstressed syllables, or of including more than one unstressed with a stressed

[5] *De Arte metrica, Opera Omnia,* Tomus Primus, Migne *Patrologiae Latinae* (Paris, 1862), Tomus 90, 173: "Videtur autem rhythmus metris esse consimilis, quae est verborum modulata compositio non metrica ratione, sed numero syllabarum ad judicium aurium examinata, ut sunt carmina vulgarium poetarum. Et quidem rhythmus sine metro esse potest, metrum vero sine rhythmo esse non potest."

syllable. Line V.21.7 contains regular alternation of stressed and unstressed:

Nu man wízinot then mán,   ther armen sélidono irbán:
   Now that man receives his pay   who did the poor a roof
                                    gainsay.

the following line continues with a surplus of unaccented syllables:

ist férro irdríban fon hímile úz,   ther anderemo nímist sinaz
                                                hús!
   far from heaven he is driven out,   who from another
                                            takes his house!

Others, like 1.18.9*b, lioht ana finstri*, contain only one unaccented syllable, a few lines none. Apparently Otfrid strove for a meter like that of V.21.7 and assumed its requirements were satisfied by lines containing four stressed syllables, whether or not these were accompanied by unstressed. Small wonder that he could adopt intact lines from alliterative poems. Reading the late Old High German alliterative verse with his accentual and rhythmical principles, Otfrid could probably have fitted it all into his metrical system. Accordingly the difference between Otfrid's rhythm and that of his Old High German predecessors lies primarily in theory and secondarily in practice. Otfrid chose as model for his verse the meters of the Latin writers, but his admiration for them was less instrumental in making the shift to metric patterns than was the changing Old High German language.

The way for the utilization of rime as binding element in verse had also been prepared by linguistic developments. As pointed out in Chapter 3, stress had shifted from nouns to syntactic elements; the Old Saxon *Genesis* poet even introduces verbs into his metrically important syllables. And the end of sentences was often more heavily stressed than the beginning, as is evident from the long anacruses in the *Heliand,* or such lines aş the following in the *Muspilli,* 89:

dara quimit ze deru rihtungu   so vilo dia dar ar resti arstent.
　　there come to the judgment   as many as stand up from
　　　　　　　　　　　　　　　　　　　　　　　their rest.

the chief stress of the first half-line falls on the very last word, that of the second on the two last words. Such linguistic shifts can scarcely have failed to suggest the advantage of rime over alliteration in connecting the half-lines.

We may assume that the new sentence stress pattern was apparent to poets before Otfrid, for rime is not entirely absent in any of the older alliterative works, even in such purely Germanic forms as the charms or in works that maintain a strict alliterative line, such as the *Beowulf.* In Germany it is both ornamental, as in the tag incorporated in the *Wessobrunn Prayer, enteo ni uuenteo* "end nor limit," or structural, replacing alliteration, as in the last line of the first Merseburg charm: *insprinc haptbandun,   invar vigandun.* In England rime does not advance beyond the ornamental level until after the time of Otfrid. Even in the *Battle of Maldon,* it is used for only a limited structural purpose, for indicating larger divisions of the poem. Only in the *Chronicle* poem on the death of Alfred, in 1036, do we find rime replacing alliteration, as it had two centuries earlier in Germany. But not for another century and a half does it replace alliteration entirely in the main stream of English poetry: Layamon, about 1200, still alternated between alliteration and rime; his successors, however, turned exclusively to the use of rime.

English poetry, accordingly, carried out slowly and gradually a change in poetic technique that Otfrid accomplished by imitating Latin poetry. His break with the past was not complete; rime was not unknown before him in Germanic verse. But his sustained use of it throughout a long poem must be

174

credited as an important innovation in the history of Germanic poetic form.

Otfrid's *Krist,* then, modified the borrowed epic form in a twofold manner : by carrying through end rime, and by regularization of rhythm, or in Bede's words, by the introduction of meter. Other Old High German poetry shows us that these were not learned innovations, introduced only in the cells of Otfrid's cloister; for although distribution of Otfrid's poem was limited, none of the later High German literature reverts to the alliterative tradition. Of the two innovations, the regularization of the rhythm was probably the less revolutionary, for subsequent Old High German poems resemble Otfrid's in rhythm more than in rime. The new rhythms were provided by the language; a stock of rimes could only be acquired in time—Otfrid's is still very small. Further evidence that Otfrid's writings have their roots in popular traditions is provided by study of his vocabulary. His psychological terms more nearly resemble the Middle High German terms than do those of learned writers such as Notker, who were producing pedagogical and scientific treatises. Consequently, although it may appear at first sight that Otfrid introduced quite foreign features into Germanic poetry, upon further examination it is clear that his innovations were not out of keeping with contemporary trends and that the features he borrowed from Latin verse had been prepared for in the language.

The following centuries, disrupted by unsettled political conditions, such as the invasions of the Hungarians, and by changes within the monastic world, such as the Cluniac reforms, did not foster assimilation of Otfrid's innovations. Poets of the following centuries continued to strive for regular meters, but made little headway with rimes, as may be illustrated by the twelfth-century High German poem, *Judith.* In each of its four occurrences in the genuine parts of the

175

poem, *Holoferni* rimes with *gerni,* and the rhythm is no better than that of Otfrid, as may be illustrated by the opening couplet of the poem:

Ein kuninc hîz Holoferni,
der streit widir goti gerni.
  Holofernes a king was hight,
  who against God loved to fight.

Yet only poetic genius, spurred on by a second period of imitating the strict rhythm and variety of rime of Romance poetry, was required to remove the remaining shortcomings of these lines, and to employ rime and rhythm for its own purposes, as Gottfried does in his toying introduction to *Tristan und Îsolt,* for example, lines 237 ff.:

Ir leben, ir tôt sint unser brôt.
sus lebet ir leben, sus lebet ir tôt.
sus lebent sie noch und sint doch tôt:
und ist ir tôt der lebenden brôt.
  Though live, though dead, they are our bread.
  as lives their life, so live they dead.
  so live they yet and still are dead
  and to the living they dead are bread.

Gottfried's rimed couplets should scarcely be compared with those of Otfrid, or even with those of Gottfried's immediate predecessors. To fulfill his aim of producing in suitable dress a German epic on the life of Christ, Otfrid had to restrict his language, even to the point of introducing grammatical solecisms; for Gottfried, however, almost any phrasing, rhythm or rimes were possible that might support his story.

Neither in Old English nor in Old Norse was the change from alliterative to rimed verse as abrupt as in Old High German; both maintained alliterative verse long after the introduction of rime. Except for the retention of alliterative verse, and for a longer period of development, the change from alliteration to rime in England parallels that in Ger-

many. In the north the addition of rime followed a different
course; from the ninth century end rime might accompany
alliteration as a structural feature of Skaldic verse, but remained secondary to it until the fourteenth century. Its introduction will be discussed further below, together with other
formal characteristics of Skaldic verse.

Examples of rimes supplementing alliteration in Old
English have been given above. Some of these extend on-
ward from the stem syllable, as the following from the Old
English *Judith* (2 and 63)

in þys ginnan grunde;   hēo þǣr þā gearwe funde
   on this gaping ground;   she there girded found
bealofull his beddes nēosan,   þǣr hē sceolde his blǣd forlēosan
   hatefully to use his bed,   where he was to forfeit his
                               head ...

We may note further that in these rimed lines the rhythm
seems almost involuntarily to be alternating. When rime not
merely supplements alliteration but has replaced it, as in the
poem on the death of Alfred in the *Anglo-Saxon Chronicle,*
the rimed couplet requires no further struggle; it has become
established in English verse. Between these lines from the
Chronicle poem (3–4)

sume hi man wið feo sealde,   sume hreowlice acwealde,
sume hi man bende,   sume hi man blende,
   some of them they sold for fee,   others they killed
                                     miserably,
   some of them they bind,   some of them they blind,

and St. Godric's *Hymn to the Virgin* of the following century,
only a greater regularity had been introduced:

Sainte Marie, Cristes bur
Maidenes clenhad, moderes flur,
Dilie mine sinne, rixe in min mod,
Bring me to winne wið self God.

177

Sainted Mary, Christ's own bower,
Maiden's purity, Mother's flower,
Wipe out my sin, rule in my mind,
May joy with God himself I find.

When Chaucer turned to French poetry as his model, as had the twelfth- and thirteenth-century German poets, his innovations in form continued and carried to perfection the trend towards a regular rhythm. Following the French original, Chaucer maintained four accents in lines of even rhythm in his translation of the *Romaunt of the Rose*. In view of Chaucer's great prestige even rhythm was thereafter observed by English poets. Through Chaucer, as through the great Middle High German poets two centuries earlier, the new form which was being introduced in the course of several centuries was brought to perfection. Linguistic changes had removed the basis for alliterative verse in southern England, as in Germany, and had gradually led to an alternating rhythm which was completely regularized when the poets came into contact with the stricter Romance forms.

Besides regularity of rhythm the Germanic lyric poets found in France also a conscious variety of stanza forms. On the basis of these Chaucer introduced complex forms, such as the ballade and the roundel. In Germany the influence of France came two centuries earlier and was not confined to the introduction of a variety of involved stanza patterns: the entire structure of the stanza was redesigned as a tripartite unit, and henceforward stanzas of whatever shape were put into this mold.

Between the Old High German period and the early twelfth century the High German lyric had remained at the level of the epic: rhythm was clumsy and not carried beyond the half-line; anacrusis of one or more syllables was introduced at will; impure rimes were not avoided. Further, as late as the twelfth century lyrics were limited to one stanza. These

features of form may be illustrated in the following anonymous poem from the early twelfth century, and in the early
poems cited in the preceding chapter (*MF* 3.18) :

Mich dunket niht sô guotes   noch sô lobesam
sô diu liehte rôse   und die minne mînes man.
diu kleinen vogellîne
diu singent in dem walde :   dêst menegem herzen liep.
mirn kome mîn holder geselle,   in hân der sumerwünne niet.

    I think there's nought as good   nor worth praise enough
    as the lovely rose   and my own lover's love.
    the tiny cheerful birds,
    they warble in the forest :   that's many a heart's cheer.
unless my dear comrade come,   no summer-joys I'll share.

Such was the German lyric poetry before it was modified by the Provençal lyric. The somewhat later English lyric,
Sainte Marie, cited above, exhibits the same simple form,
with less irregular rhythm and less irregular lines. Provençal
influence extended to content as well as form. In the German
love lyrics composed before the Provençal poetry was imitated, as in this poem, love is a simple attraction between man
and woman, and if thwarted, other pleasures, such as those
in nature, are blunted, especially for the woman. In the Provençal tradition love is a complicated social convention, the
chief aim of which is yearning, usually of the male for his
unapproachable mistress. These conventions and the forms in
which they were expressed, the German poets adopted at the
end of the twelfth century, and with them the devotion of the
poet to his art. The practice of Provençal love poetry was
virtually a cult. The spark which raised this poetry to a stimu-
lating level and caused it to sweep Europe has been greatly
sought, but is as obscure as that which raised the English
mystery plays to the level of Marlowe, Shakespeare, and Jon-
son, but whose absence left at its pedestrian level the contemporary German drama. Roots of the Provençal lyric may,

179

however, be found in various cultural influences converging in South France in the eleventh century: Arabic and other oriental influences; religious mysticism; Mariolatry; Latin lyrics; rediscovery of Ovid; social surroundings in courts with the master absent on Crusades or other warfare: all these were combined with a native love lyric. As a result of the new conventions the object of love was set on a pedestal, and one or more poets could worship her from afar. Content from the first was stereotyped, as indicated in the preceding chapter. Form accordingly gained in importance, for to bring the highest praise to his lady the poets had to be zealous in fulfilling external requirements. To outdo their competitors they invented a form as complex as possible. Even greater honor redounded to the lady if the poet never re-used a form. These motives led in the eleventh century to great exactness, complexity, and variety of form among the Provençal poets, and these formal principles with the courtly conventions were taken over in Germany by the minnesingers.

The earliest German minnesongs were composed about 1170, the time of the birth of their greatest writer, Walther von der Vogelweide. Almost at once form was as perfect as was that of the poets imitated, as may be noted from the poem of Von Husen cited above. Walther's predecessor and teacher, Reinmar, achieved the technical excellence of Provençal poetry; with formal mastery Walther combined variety of subject matter. The modifications in matter brought into Germanic poetry from Provençal do not concern us further here; those in form are thoroughgoing, completing the changes which separate present Germanic poetry so distinctly from that in the alliterative form, as is evident by comparing with the above anonymous poem any of Walther's poems, such as those cited above or the following (this is generally considered to be the third stanza of the poem, *So die bluomen,* cited above, p. 60):

180

Nû wol dan, welt ir die wârheit schouwen!
gên wir zuo des meien hôhgezîte!
der ist mit aller sîner krefte komen.
  seht an in und seht an schœne frouwen,
wederz dâ daz ander überstrîte:
daz bezzer spil, ob ich daz hân genomen.
  owê der mich dâ welen hieze,
deich daz eine dur daz ander lieze,
wie rehte schiere ich danne kür!
hêr Meie, ir müeset merze sîn,
ê ich mîn frowen dâ verlür.

     Ah well, if you would see the truth aright,
     then come now to the holiday of May;
     he with all his majesty is here.
      Look at him and look at women bright,
     which of them the other would o'erweigh,
     that the poorer choice I'd make I fear.
      Alas if I be forced to choose;
     that for the one, the other I should lose;
     how quickly then my choice I'd take,
     Sir May, you'd have to be as March
     before my lady I'd forsake.

This poem of Walther's may illustrate how the German poets learned from Romance verse to construct forms extending beyond a long line, and to give poems consisting of more than one stanza formal unity. Repetition of the rhythmic pattern and rime schemes in the first two sections, or stollen, effected a continuous structure through external form alone; the stollen were often linked to the *abgesang* through similar rhythm, or even through rimes repeated from the stollen, as in Walther's poem, *Ich bin nû sô rehte frô,* 118.24. Further stanzas might be linked with the first through repetition of the form, as in the poem cited above, or through matching of a rime only in successive stanzas, as Walther's rime *meisterinne,* 55.32, is not matched until *küniginne,* 56.12.

    After Germanic poetry had undergone such influence from Romance, the attention of the audience to form was no longer focused on the technical competence with which a single line was constructed. Now the audience could not fail to perceive longer formal segments, even in poems not constructed on the tripartite pattern. On hearing a poem like Walther's dealing with the seasons the audience would know after one stanza that Walther required seven identical rimes on the same vowel, e.g., 76.1 :

Die tôren sprechent sniâ snî,
die armen liute owê owî.
ich bin swære alsam ein blî.
der wintersorge hân ich drî:
swaz der unt der andern sî,
der wurde ich alse schiere frî,
wær uns der sumer nâhe bî.

    The fools now say, "there's snow, there's snow."
    Poor people merely: "oh my oh."
    Lead could not press me so low.
    In winter, triple is my woe:
    Though one sorrow I might show,
    Quickly from my mind they'd go
    If just the summer weren't so slow!

Much of the poem's formal appeal would result from hearing how successful Walther would be in finding adequate rimes for the other vowels and in maintaining the form he had chosen. These two stanzas of Walther may show how Germanic poets had learned from Romance poetry to give their poems, stanzas, and subdivisions of stanzas adequate formal characteristics.

Now, too, variety of structure was possible. Lines were no longer confined to three or four stresses, repeated over and over, but could contain as few as one stress or as many as eight. Only the taste of the poet determined their length. Yet once a fixed length was chosen it was repeated in the corresponding line of another stanza. The only limitation on stanza form was that it consist of three sections if in the favorite tripartite form; the length of the sections, or their relative proportions, was not fixed. Furthermore, great variety of rime and rhythm could be achieved. Virtually any rime scheme might be followed, *abc abc de de, ab ab cddc, ab ab acc,* etc., or lines might be left unrimed in their own stanza or even in the poem. Rhythmic variation might be introduced by the use of anacrusis in one line, but not in the next, with a succession of lines in either iambic or trochaic, and even dactylic rhythm. Each line, however, was cast in one rhythm, and the matching line of a subsequent stollen or stanza continued in it.

From Romance verse the German poets accordingly learned how to introduce freedoms in sections of form that earlier were fixed, and conversely how other limitations in form would permit them to extend their formal subdivisions. The introduction of the new freedoms fostered great variety in form, so that the tripartite structure was scarcely a limitation. Furthermore, linguistic changes had eliminated many unstressed syllables so that the requirement of fixed rhythm, or meter, was not difficult to fulfill. In Romance verse accordingly the German lyric poets of the late twelfth and the thirteenth centuries found patterns that permitted them to apply the rhythmic niceties of their language in delicately molded stanzaic forms that hitherto were unknown in Germanic poetry.

A departure from the simpler Germanic forms was made by the skalds much earlier in the north. Contemporaneous with our oldest Eddic poetry are the first Skaldic poems ascribed to Bragi. Neither can be dated earlier than the ninth century. By this time the Vikings had learned to know peoples of Europe who had adopted the Christian-Roman culture: the Irish, the English, the French, and others less intimately. The Viking forms in the plastic arts such as the carvings on their boat prows and the ornaments for their women were borrowed from these peoples, chiefly from the Irish. To the foreign contacts, primarily the Irish, some scholars therefore ascribe the characteristics of Skaldic form. Since the marauding Vikings, of whom the skalds themselves were not the gentlest, made it their mission to obliterate churches and monasteries, and with them most contemporary records, we have only secondary evidence on which to base our conclusions. And this secondary evidence has been variously viewed, not always without glasses befogged by misguided patriotism.

The most vigorous and persistent scholar to contend that Skaldic poetry was simply a native development was the Icelander Finnur Jónsson. He argued that for poetic influence to be exerted the groups in question had to live side by side in amity for a lengthy period. This the Vikings and Irish rather obviously did not do. Accordingly Jónsson needs to investigate no further; since to his mind cultural conditions did not favor borrowing, the alternative theory must be chosen. It cannot be maintained, however, that Jónsson's stipulations for borrowing must be fulfilled before borrowing takes place. The Middle High German lyric poets, for example, did an excellent job of borrowing Provençal forms in an exceedingly short time though their contacts with the French were restricted to tournaments, festivals, or to contacts between individuals; political relations between the medieval Germans and French were hardly more amicable than those between the North Germanic peoples and the Irish. The North Germanic peoples borrowed Celtic and English motifs in the other arts even earlier when contacts were much more sporadic, and no more peaceful. It would be little more difficult for a poet to learn a poetic form from a captive and adapt it to his language than for a draftsman to copy a finely embossed shield and adapt the patterns to other work. Moreover, the Irish chroniclers have left evidence of a not wholly superficial cultural contact, for they have preserved Norse names in the various forms through which they developed. If the Irish knew the Norse well enough to record intimate phonetic details of their speech, the Norse should also have had opportunities to become acquainted with the much-practiced Irish song. Irish annals report the first large Viking raid in the year 617. Two centuries later there were Norse settlements in Ireland, for example at Dublin, providing opportunities for intimate contact, and even intermarriage. Some of the saga heroes boast an Irish princess among their ancestors, for example, Kjartan in the *Laxdale Saga*. Other reports tell of freedmen and maids of Irish birth, such as those brought by Auð to Iceland in the ninth century.[6] Since similar opportunities for getting to know Celtic culture were provided in Britain, we find no need to assume for Old Norse poetry the parochiality that Jónsson propounded.

Scholars of the other school, of whom possibly the most influential was Bugge, base their reasons for assuming that Skaldic poetry was borrowed rather than independently developed on the similarities between Skaldic and Irish verse and on the dissimilarities between Skaldic and Eddic verse. Mossé[7] finds the following five differences between early Skaldic and Eddic poetry:

1. Skaldic poetry requires a fixed number of syllables per line; the Eddic line is free.

2. Skaldic poetry uses rimes and systems of rimes; Eddic poetry none.

3. Skaldic poetry groups stanzas; Eddic poetry makes no such groups.

4. Skaldic poetry has a number of particular meters; Eddic poetry at most has three.

[6] *Landnámabók,* Íslendinga sögur, ed. Guðni Jónsson (Reykjavik, 1942), sec. 146, 81.

[7] F. Mossé, "Skothending," *Studia Germanica,* Lunder germanistische Forschungen (Lund, 1934), 242–50.

5. Skaldic poetry contains an abundance of metaphors, most Eddic poetry only a few.

Further characteristics of Skaldic poetry are:[8]

6. Interlocking syntax patterns;

7. Avoidance of anacrusis, especially in the second half-line;

8. Feminine cadences at the end of lines;

9. Preference for monosyllabic drops and monosyllabic anacrusis.

All these characteristics, though sporadic in Eddic poetry, are found in Irish verse after the eighth century. Hence scholars of the Bugge school assume that they were borrowed from Irish to Norse.

Some weighty arguments from the history of the Celts and Germans may be cited in their favor. We know from sources such as Caesar's *De bello gallico* that the Celts and Germans long lived side-by-side, and that at this time the Celts enjoyed cultural superiority over the Germans. Therefore, when we know that the institution of court poets was long established among the Celts, but totally absent among the Germans until the time of the skalds, it is credible that this institution was adopted from the Celts. Furthermore, Bugge's observation that one of the earliest Skaldic poets composed a genealogical poem—a genre totally lacking in Germanic poetry but highly favored in Celtic verse—lends support to the theory of Celtic influence. Bugge's school accordingly has some strong arguments in its favor, though not enough to overwhelm its opponents.

Possibly the cause of our greatest difficulty in arriving at a satisfactory decision in favor of either school is our ignorance of cultural conditions and interrelations in early Scandinavia, Ireland, and England. For all these areas our information is meager during the period before the ninth

[8] Heusler, *Die altgermanische Dichtung,* 113.

century, the time when Skaldic as well as Eddic poetry apparently was fully developed. Furthermore, only a fraction of the Eddic and Skaldic poems have come down to us. Features that seem to be purely Celtic and Skaldic may therefore have been found in some of the lost Eddic poetry. On the other hand, we cannot simply assume that such features were native Germanic though we find identical formal features in non-Skaldic verse and in the Skaldic; Celtic influence may already have left its stamp on the apparently native Germanic poetry. Eddic poetry may have been subject to the same influence as Skaldic, as may also the other Germanic alliterative poetry. The England in which the *Beowulf* was composed was under strong Irish influence. And Irish monks were even in Germany long before any of our German verse was written down.

There is further the slight possibility that the features common to Celtic and Germanic verse were borrowed from Germanic. The Celtic poets were not averse to borrowing, to the extent of abandoning their native system of poetry for features from the Latin hymns that are common to both Celtic and Skaldic verse—syllable-counting, use of rimes, variety of meters. The numerous metaphors and the interlocking syntax patterns, however, are found already in the older Celtic verse. The following stanza, which K. Meyer dates in the eighth century,[9] may be cited as an early illustration of the interweaving of native Celtic and of Latin elements in Irish verse:

Badhbrī cūicid Ērenn uile,   ard bara, brass bile,
dobādi sīs, ni sīd chena,   cach rīg acht Rīg nime.

The translation is an adaption of his German rendition:

> The battle-king of the entire province of Ireland,
>   a noble terror, a mighty tree;

[9] K. Meyer, *Bruchstücke der älteren Lyrik Irlands,* Abhandlungen der preussischen Akademie der Wissenschaften. Phil.-Hist. Kl. Nr. 7 (Berlin, 1919), 7.

> every king he destroys—without that no peace—
> only not the king of heaven.

In this poem which predates Bragi, we note elements borrowed from the Latin: the fixed number of syllables (with monosyllabic drops and anacrusis), the rimes, added to the elements present in earlier Irish verse, alliteration, the feminine cadences, abundance of metaphors, and interlocking syntax. We might assume that if the Celtic poets so readily abandoned their own forms for the Latin, they may also have adopted from the Germanic additional poetic ornamentation. Yet this assumption is improbable. Celtic traditions suggest a flourishing literature as early as the beginning of our era. Some very early lyric poems have come down to us without rime and without a fixed number of syllables from before the time of the Latin influence. Hence, we can almost without question eliminate the possibility of Celtic borrowing from Germanic.

In dealing with the problem of the origin of Skaldic poetry, we must, in consequence of our lack of early materials, rely greatly on methodology and on a comparison of Skaldic with other forms of Germanic poetry. The earliest poems from the various Germanic languages may also give us evidence for making assumptions. Since the time of the greatest part of the controversy between the Jónsson and the Bugge schools a runic stone has been dug up on which is inscribed a difficult, but, apart from damaged sections, complete, short Germanic poem. The inscription, found at Eggjum in West Norway, may be dated approximately A.D. 650. Our next earliest Germanic poems were composed in England. These we may examine for features similar to those in Skaldic poetry, judging them from the peculiar method of work of the Skaldic poets, and from the impact of other poetic systems on Germanic poetry elsewhere.

When we examine these common features we must not

forget that the skalds were highly conscious artists, schooling and training themselves in their craft; in their own terms, to write poetry was to *yrkja* 'work', not merely to wait for inspiration. Further, the skalds restricted themselves to occasional poetry dealing with a limited number of themes. In these self-imposed limitations of form and subject we must examine their employment and development of poetic devices.

Possibly the element of Skaldic poetry which seems most unlike Germanic poetry is the fixed number of syllables per line. As we have noted above, the Germanic alliterative line, on which Skaldic verse is based, fixed only the number of stressed syllables; the unstressed were virtually unregulated in number, so that, as in the Gallehus horn inscription, they could vary between one and three per stressed syllable, and elsewhere even more widely. In Skaldic poetry we find the unstressed regulated as well as the stressed.

But the principle is not that of Latin, or Celtic, verse. In these, syllables were counted, and limited, regardless of their quantity or stress. In the Skaldic poetry the Germanic principle of equivalence was never given up; some lines of a poem in which four syllables were standard might contain five (two of them short and equivalent to one long), as in the second line of Egil's *Hǫfuðlausn: en ek Viðris ber*. Latin and Celtic verse, on the other hand, counted every syllable that was not elided.

Moreover, Skaldic verse maintained the uneven rhythms of alliterative poetry. Three stressed syllables per line were normal in the *dróttkvætt* line of six syllables. A stressed syllable might be accompanied by one, two, three, or no unstressed syllables; the total number of unstressed syllables in one line were required to equal the number of stressed, but their distribution was unregulated. In the first line of Egil's *Hǫfuðlausn* two unstressed syllables accompany the first stressed, in the second but one:

189

Vestr fórk of ver,
en ek Viðris ber.

The Skaldic rhythmic units accordingly are not unlike those
found in Eddic verse. The reduction in number of unstressed
syllables, modifications which the Germanic alliterative line
underwent in the north as the result of linguistic changes,
has been described above. Theoretically, the northern Eddic
poets might still employ a great number of unstressed syllables per stressed syllables, but generally they did not. Many
lines are restricted to one unstressed per stressed syllable, as
Song of Weland 19:

Nú berr Boðvildr   brúðar minnar—
biðka ek þess bót!—   bauga rauða!
    Now Boðvild wears   my bride's—
    recompense I await not—red-gold ring.

The syllabic restrictions of the skalds differ therefore
in notable details from the syllable-counting of Latin and Irish
poetry. Rather than explaining it as an importation, we may
view it as a further extension of the trend found in Eddic
poetry to limit the number of unstressed syllables in the line.

The use of rimes, on the other hand, was sporadic in
old Germanic and Eddic poetry. But in our earliest Skaldic
poem the system is virtually full-blown. Though Bragi followed no fixed system in his use of *aðalhendings* and *skothendings,* in the verse of his successors odd-numbered lines
contain *skothendings,* even lines *aðalhendings.* Such internal
rimes are widely used elsewhere only in poetry written by the
Irish. While they adopted rime from the Latin hymns, there
only end syllables rimed. But even in the Latin poetry written
by the Irish we find internal rime, both designed to bind the
two short lines of a long line, as in the following hymn to
Mary:[10]

    [10] This is taken from W. Meyer, "Die Verskunst der Iren in rhyth-
mischen Lateinischen Gedichten," *Gesammelte Abhandlungen zur mittella-*

Maria, mater miranda,   patrem suum edidit.
per quem aqua late lo*tus*   *totus* mundus credidit. . . .

or within the first short line of a long line, itself the second
of a pair:

pro qua s*ani* Christi*ani*   vendunt sua omnia.

Apparently the Irish adapted Latin rime to this use, just as
they had expanded the final end-syllable rime of the Latin
hymns to a bisyllabic rime.

But in Germanic such use of rime is rare outside Skaldic
poetry. It is probably most prominent in the *Valkyrialióð*, a
poem of the late tenth century which is contained in *Njáls
saga;* though composed in Eddic form this contains Skaldic
hendings:

Vel kváðom vér   um kon*ung ung*an
sigrhlióða fiǫlð;   syngiom heilar.
E*nn* hi*nn* nemi,   er h*eyri* á,
geirfl*ióð*a hl*ióð*   ok gumnom segi.

Both *skothendings* and *aðalhendings* are used here, but un-
systematically and not only in syllables with the chief stress.
Skothendings, which we expect to find in odd lines, are used
in 5 and 6; *aðalhendings,* in 2 and 7. From this poem, however, we can hardly determine native Germanic elements, for
it deals with a situation in Ireland and may even have been
composed there, and thus the abundance of *hendings* might
rather lend weight to the theory that they were borrowed
from the Irish.

Less expected possibly is the use of *hendings* in such an
old Germanic poem as the *Beowulf*, e.g., 322 hring*ī*ren sc*ī*r.
F. Kluge found twenty-eight *aðalhendings* and almost a hun-

---

teinischen Rythmik, III (Berlin, 1936), 303–46, where a fuller discussion
may be found.

dred *skothendings* in the *Beowulf*,[11] and *hendings* in other Old English poetry as well; inasmuch as they were more frequently used in the early Old English verse than in the late, he assumes that they were purely Germanic in origin. Such rimes, Kluge believes, were suggested by the Germanic initial stress. Yet, while earlier and non-Skaldic poetry contains *hendings,* we do not find them used systematically outside of Skaldic poetry. Though lines like *Beowulf* 322 indicate that rimes were available as poetic ornamentation in Germanic, their regular application and structural use so parallel the use of rimes in Irish verse that they make somewhat unlikely the theory of completely independent Germanic development. Although the other distinguishing marks of Skaldic verse were not exploited in non-Skaldic verse to the extent that they are found in the Skaldic, they are by no means foreign there either.

Grouping, when present in Skaldic poems, as in the *drápa,* is brought about through repetition of a single line or more, usually after a fixed number of stanzas. As an example we might note Egil's *Hǫfudlausn,* where the last two lines of the sixth stanza are repeated as the last two lines of the ninth, the last two of the twelfth as the last two of the fifteenth in a poem of twenty stanzas. Such repetitions, less regular to be sure, are found in other Germanic poetry, with possibly the repeated question of the *Vǫluspá* as the most notable:

vitoð ér enn, eða hvat?
Do you know something more?

this is found at the end of stanzas 27, 28, 33, 35, 39, 41, 48, 62, and 63. In Old English verse we find in *Deor's Lament* the following line repeated as lines 7, 13, 17, 20, 27, 42:

[11] "Zur Geschichte des Reimes im Altgermanischen," *PBB,* 9 (1884), 422–50.

Þæs oferēode,   þisses swā mæg.
    That passed away,   this may too.

Missing from non-Skaldic verse, therefore, is only the regular recurrence and restriction to specific types of poems such as the solemn *drápa,* not the use of repeated lines.

The various Skaldic meters which Snorri lists in the *Háttatal* differ among themselves primarily in nonmetrical characteristics, in use of rime, distribution of *hendings,* rhetorical and syntactic practices. From a purely metrical point of view there is no great variety. The favorite form is the *dróttkvætt* with its line of six syllables. With Sievers we may assume that this line is derived from the normal Germanic alliterative line by the addition of two syllables; for the greatest number of *dróttkvætt* lines end in bisyllables, and if we read the lines without these we find the old rhythmic patterns. Since the skalds introduced a great variety of stanzas by rearranging other characteristics of their form, it seems fair to assume that they might have modified their lines by varying the number of accents per line. Sievers suggests that all the Skaldic lines are based on the Germanic line:[12] the four-syllable line as in Egil's *Hǫfuðlausn,* is the simple line itself, the six-syllable line an expanded form, and the eight-syllable line an expanded form of this: less common types of lines are derived from the two latter by the loss of syllables. While the variety of metric structure is greater in Skaldic than in other Germanic verse, it does not compare with that in Celtic verse. The northern popular poetry had evolved a number of varied forms, the *málaháttr* and *ljóðaháttr* beside the *fornyrðislag,* and it is not unreasonable to assume that the skalds continued the inventiveness.

Kennings are characteristic of Skaldic poetry by their abundance and complexity, not by their presence. For they are found in all Germanic verse, and, though possibly by ac-

[12] *Altgermanische Metrik* (Halle, 1893), 98–118, 239–42.

193

cident, in Germanic proper names, such as *Hildebrand* 'battle-torch (sword)'. Their ultimate origin may be a problem, but this is of no concern for their characteristic use in Skaldic verse. For the kenning in the Eggjum stone poem, *náseo* 'body-sea, blood', and the presence of kennings in the southern as well as in the northern verse establishes them as elements of verse in the time of Germanic unity. Kennings to be sure abound also in the Celtic song of praise, as may be illustrated in the initial stanza of a poem which K. Meyer ascribes to the eighth century;[13] the translation is adapted from Meyer:

Indrechtach īath m briūin
bresfota, bailc baind,
breo derg di chlaind
cēt rīg, roart caur,
cāinfāel ilchonda
ave muirne muin.

> I of Brian's lands
> Battle-mighty, strong in deed,
> red flame from a race
> of hundred kings, great hero,
> a stately violent wolf,
> grandson of Muirenn the Worthy.

Here, however, the kennings are employed differently from those in Skaldic verse; they are appositional while those in the Skaldic poems are independent; further, they lack the complexity of the Skaldic kennings. Both of these differences are apparent in virtually any selections. In the first stanza of Egil's *Hǫfuðlausn* 'the sea of Odin's breast' is an involved kenning for poetry, which rests on the story that the art of poetry was obtained by Odin from a giantess in the form of mead. A similar kenning in the first stanza of Einar's *Vellekla,* 'the lore of Kvasir's gore', stands for Skaldic poetry; the capability to write Skaldic poetry is again imparted as a

[13] K. Meyer, *Über die älteste irische Dichtung,* Abhandlungen der königlichen preussischen Akademie der Wissenschaften. Phil.-Hist. Kl. Nr. 10 (Berlin, 1914), 25.

drink, now the blood of Kvasir. In neither selection, nor in the Eggjum inscription, is the kenning further explained as are those in Celtic verse. Accordingly, while the kenning may have been borrowed around the beginning of our era from Celtic, its characteristic use in Skaldic verse can hardly be derived from the kenning of Celtic verse.

The other characteristics of Skaldic poetry we also find in Eddic poetry, though like the kenning they are less complex in the simpler verse and less consistently maintained. For a pattern of interrupted syntax we may compare the section cited above from the nineteenth stanza of the *Song of Weland*. In Skaldic verse the interruptions were more elaborate, often carried over into several lines, but essentially no different from that of the *Song of Weland*.

Avoidance of anacrusis in the second half-lines we also find in Eddic verse. The *Song of Weland* exhibits anacrusis here in approximately one out of three lines, the *Þrymskviða* in one out of four. Feminine cadences again are preferred in the Eddic poetry. Approximately seven out of eight lines in the *Song of Weland* have such endings, approximately six out of seven in the *Þrymskviða*. Ample evidence has been given above that the Eddic poets, like the skalds, preferred monosyllabic drops.

Of the various characteristics which have been ascribed to Skaldic verse all but rime have been found widespread in other Germanic verse. It is hardly necessary therefore to look outside the Germanic area for a source for most of the characteristic elements of the Skaldic verse. Poets as self-conscious as the skalds in their art and as careful in molding their form, favoring certain elements of pre-existent Germanic poetry may have regularized these and limited their occurrence. In Chapter 4 we have noted that the Middle High German courtly poets, who were similar to the skalds both in attention to form and in lack of interest in new subject matter, selected

195

elements in the form of their predecessors and made them dominant in their works. We may assume a similar manner of work among the skalds. Just as Konrad generalized external formal features to the point where he was unable to maintain normal syntax patterns, so the skalds, encouraged by their highly trained audiences, may have striven for ever more refined regularity in rhythm and in meters, and for more involved kennings, with consequent disregard of the syntax patterns of the colloquial. Such self-conscious artists would have been able to select from a foreign poetry a striking formal feature like the *hendings* and adapt them to their verse, as the Middle High German poets borrowed the tripartite form. In the main then, the characteristics of Skaldic verse must not be sought in borrowing fom Celtic, but rather in the social setting of the skalds and of their verse.

The assumption that the earliest skalds, rather than importing Irish forms, selected and developed for their poetry formal features of earlier Germanic verse that struck their fancy may be supported by the absence of formal elements which are mandatory in Irish verse. The end of an Irish poem is marked by repetition of a part or of all of the first line. In Skaldic verse this neat device is as completely absent as is the Irish principle of syllable-counting. Further, throughout Skaldic poetry the principle of alliteration is the same as that of Germanic, not of Irish, verse. If Skaldic form were based on that of Irish verse we might expect in it some of the non-Germanic formal traits common in Irish poetry. The similarity between Skaldic and earlier Germanic forms on the other hand suggests that the highly conscious Skaldic artists molded a new Germanic form primarily from selected elements that were less rigorously utilized in earlier northern verse.

When we review the changes in form which resulted from changes in influence we note either that these pertain to larger segments of form or that they bring to a conclusion changes which had been inherited previously. Nowhere do we find support for assuming that the essential modifications of small segments such as the poetic line are the results of importations.

Larger segments of form were imported into Germanic verse in two different periods: in the eighth century, the epic; in the twelfth, the lyric. The imported elements affect epic form secondarily through their modifications of material, for they concern themselves with expansion of setting, of historical background, and of the personality of the hero; through expansion of these elements poetic form is amplified. The element imported into the twelfth-century lyric was structural; German poets now took over the tripartite division of the lyric stanza.

More constant is the impact of non-Germanic forms which brought to perfection formal trends initiated by linguistic changes. In ninth-century Germany Otfrid strove on the basis of Latin models to regularize completely the smoothed rhythms which his language was providing for him. English poets made similar efforts a few centuries later. Moreover, Otfrid and the later English poets found rime more suitable for their languages which were stressing less the initial elements of form classes such as the nouns, but instead were placing the important stresses on sentence and phrase final elements.

Measured by the changes which poetic forms underwent in the south, the Skaldic verse form may be ascribed rather to the social surroundings in which it flourished than to importation from the Irish. For all of its characteristic elements are extensions of elements that were present in earlier northern verse. And we find the observation generally valid for Germanic poetry that those importations are successful that modify and supplement existing forms rather than those that are totally new.

6 CONCLUSION

In studying the history of Germanic verse form we have observed various forces guiding its development. Scarcely secondary to our interest in observing the effect of these on Germanic verse form is the question of their effect on the verse form of other peoples and an evaluation of that effect. Do we find the same forces at work in poetry in general? Can we expect to find elsewhere the relations we noted for Germanic verse between linguistic and poetic form, between the demands of the audience and poetic form, between foreign influences and native traditions? Is the effect of these forces beneficial or detrimental to verse? These questions have been touched on above, and they will be discussed only briefly here, for only after further investigations of other verse could we give answers that might be generally valid.

We can, however, tentatively state that in all poetry the relationship between linguistic and verse form is similar: linguistic form dominates over verse form, limiting the possible types of verse form and making impossible the successful use of any verse form which imposes requirements that clash with the material provided by the language. English poets, for example, have never adapted successfully some poetic forms which are readily available in other European literature, forms of works whose ideas have greatly influenced English verse. For one such form, the terza rima of the *Divine Comedy*, English lacks the abundance of feminine rimes which enable

Italian poets to use it without forcing their language or distorting their subject matter. Similarly, rhythmic differences between English with its relatively strong accent and French with its even flow of syllables seem to have favored the preference for a five-foot line, rimed or unrimed, in English, for the Alexandrine in French, and the avoidance of the other in either language. Even the much-used Provençal forms, except for the fluid sonnet structure, have failed to produce memorable verse in English. Moreover, in notable translations English verse forms are preferred over those that are not native. Successful translations into English have generally departed from the form of the original and have chosen characteristic English forms. When they are turned into English, Homeric hexameters bore us. The rhythm of English, like the rhythm of other languages, accordingly regulates verse as it regulates all other utterances and determines which verse form may be successful.

The subservience of verse form to linguistic form may be further illustrated by adaptations of earlier verse in the same language; for intervening linguistic changes may not permit ready use of the old form. As an example one may compare Pound's boisterous adaptation of the thirteenth-century poem cited here :[1]

Sumer is icumen in,
lhude sing cuccu!
Groweth sed, and bloweth med,
And springth the wude nu—
        Sing cuccu!

Pound maintains the rhythm of the original chiefly by using semi-adapted Middle English forms: *lhude, raineth, staineth;* and Middle English sentence patterns: *raineth drop*. But the key word of the earlier poem, *cuccu*, exhibits a characteristic difference between the English of 1250 and that of today:

[1] Ezra Pound, *Selected Poems* (London, 1948), 119.

199

modern English has not maintained long medial consonants. This combination Pound attempts to obtain, except in the fabricated *icummen,* by using a compound (Goddamn) which consists of elements ending and beginning with the same consonant, the only pattern in which modern English shows long consonants. Though Pound's poem may be only a parody, its success can be attributed in part to the maintenance of the old rhythm with an expression not foreign to modern colloquial English. Like poetic rhythms, the prose rhythms of a bygone day can also be recaptured only by resorting to obsolescent language, or by relying unduly on unusual contemporary patterns, as may be observed by reading the "Oxen of the Sun" episode of Joyce's *Ulysses.*[2]

Other illustrations may be found in the Celtic languages. We have mentioned earlier that when rime was taken over from Latin into Irish it was extended to stem syllables. Virtually any word that a Latin poet could choose for his rime had an inflectional ending; in many Irish words, on the other hand, the stem was the final element, so that the language alone forced the abandonment of the previous practice of limiting rime to endings. A somewhat different formal modification of verse form resulted when alliteration was borrowed from Irish into Welsh. As in the Germanic languages the initial syllables of words were accented in Irish, and the initial element of these alliterated. Welsh, however, accented the second last syllable; maintenance of the Irish principle of alliteration would have been purposeless. In Welsh, then, alliteration was extended to all consonants of a line so that all were matched in another section. The Welsh adaptation of alliteration is discussed at some length by Ruth P. Lehmann,[3] who gives the following illustration:

[2] James Joyce, *Ulysses* (New York, Modern Library, Inc., 1934), 377-421.

[3] "Henry Vaughan and Welsh Poetry: A Contrast," *Philological Quarterly,* 24 (1945), 330-42.

Cold winter, cloudy wanton, . . .

Here one may observe how the consonants *c l d w n t* are repeated in the same order in the second half of the line. Unable to gain from alliteration of initial consonants the same effect as did the Irish, the Welsh poets revised its principles to suit their linguistic form. Thus Celtic verse illustrates, like Germanic verse, that changes in linguistic structure bring about changes in verse form.

Yet the effect of linguistic changes may not be immediately felt. For a poet is also regulated by the role in which his society places him, and by his artistic aims. The Germanic poets were expected by their audiences to be exponents of the cherished ideals and forms of their time, not to be innovators. Even poets who introduced elements from abroad—as did Otfrid—made their innovations largely because their society had changed ideals, just as Otfrid's society had changed from heathen Germanic to the Christian culture. Further, the Germanic societies required of poetry a practical purpose: though Germanic ideals varied from age to age, poetry had as purpose the dissemination of those current. All the long Germanic epics were composed to transmit Christian ideals, even the *Beowulf,* though in it these ideals were communicated through pre-Christian story. Medieval courtly verse in turn glorified courtly ideals: from Hartmann's poems we learn the code of chivalry; from Gottfried's the conventions of courtly love. With such aims Germanic poets avoided forms that might alienate their audiences, and in none of the early Germanic verse does one find radical formal innovations. Poetic forms were maintained until through conflict with other formal features, such as language, they hindered the presentation of the poets' matter, or until social changes brought with them new forms. When long-standing societies maintained themselves, as at the halls of the petty Scandinavian kings from the ninth to the eleventh century, and in southern Germany from the end of the twelfth through the thirteenth century, they did not seek to amplify the possibilities of verse form by borrowing from other bodies of verse or from contemporary speech; the linguistic patterns of past ages were preserved and poetic form came to be based more and more on traditional rules.

Skaldic and courtly verse accordingly are examples illustrating that conservative societies may, for a time, withstand innovations suggested by their language and yet maintain verse of a moderately high order. When societies supporting such traditional verse collapse, however, the old verse forms are abandoned and subsequent poets find no foundation for a living verse form. The new poets lack either the audience to maintain the form of their predecessors, or the training. If they observe the rhythms of contemporary speech in the old forms, the two clash and a new verse form must be laboriously constructed, or, pale imitations may be produced, for example, *meistergesang* in Germany. But subsequent verse of significance is built on new bases. Between the collapse of courtly culture in thirteenth-century Germany and the eighteenth century, no verse of general interest was produced with the possible exception of the folk song and genres based on it, such as the hymns. Icelandic verse never regained poetic eminence after the decline of Skaldic verse and the culture supporting it. Yet, except for the eleventh and twelfth centuries, we do not find in English verse—which has continually modified its forms through remodeling them on the colloquial or on foreign forms—such long periods in which only third- and fourth-class verse was produced.

We conclude that when the language of poetry follows its own canon, when prosody permits or even requires patterns that are impossible in speech, then poetry strangles itself, as did Skaldic poetry and minnesong, and it provides no basis for a flourishing verse of subsequent generations. The history of Chinese verse supports this suggestion. With the aid of elaborate riming dictionaries, linguistic patterns of a thousand or more years ago were maintained, yielding no verse of a high level during this period of obsolescence, nor even after Chinese poets sought new foundations in modern colloquial and in other literatures. For a constant stream of capable verse, form apparently must be modified continually with the changing linguistic structure, and, though poets may choose to preserve archaic elements of vocabulary, their patterns of syntax, and their rhythm, must be that of the colloquial.

When a poetic form has departed so far from the colloquial that subsequent verse has no basis to build on, the poets who are compelled to start anew with little help from their predecessors, though not so uniformly capable and dull as many of the imitators of a past tradition, attain little eminence. Well-intentioned innovators like Otfrid are read today only for linguistic interest. Even more capable ones, like the twelfth-century Heinrich von Veldeke, who introduced the courtly epic form to Germany, are respected primarily for their contribution to their successors. For readers possessing an adequate linguistic background, the Germanic poetry which still has general interest—the best of the Old Norse Eddic and Skaldic verse, the Old English *Beowulf,* some of the short Old English and Old High German heroic lays, the Middle High German courtly epics and lyrics—was produced at some time after a poetic form had been introduced and reworked, but before it had become petrified and had lost touch with the contemporary language. Gottfried and Wolfram were preceded by Friderich von Husen and Heinrich von Veldeke; the earlier Old Norse Skaldic verse, the Old English *Beowulf,* the Old High German *Hildebrandslied* by a general Germanic tradition. The eminent poets of whom we have a fair amount of information inherited a well-developed form but did not regard it as sacrosanct. Egil wrote Skaldic verse with end rime as well as interior rime; the Old English epic poets introduced expanded lines .beside the normal lines when their language was developing away from its nominal conciseness; Gottfried exploited to the full the wealth of rimes which had been made possible in Middle High German when final vowels were reduced to unstressed *e*. The most successful poetic forms then combined the experiences of previous experimentation with individual enrichment based on the developments of contemporary speech.

Study of Germanic poetry suggests therefore that poetic form should seek its rejuvenation by constant modification according to colloquial speech. Epochs which neglect this fail to produce high poetry or a basis for subsequent high poetry. But what of the effect of foreign influences? Will they have a beneficial effect at any time? Will a good poet be able to assimilate any foreign forms whatsoever into his verse? Or can we even suggest with Hulme in his "Lecture on Modern Poetry" that newly introduced forms provide the spark for great verse, where he says: "All kinds of reasons are given by the academic critics for the efflorescence of verse at any period. But the true one is very seldom given. It is the invention or introduction of a new art form." The history of Germanic verse suggests a complex, but definite answer. Imported forms may yield inferior verse, as Otfrid's borrowed rimed verse and the Icelandic fourteenth-century verse based on Romance form, or it may yield excellent verse, such as the Middle High German courtly lyric and epic based on Romance models. Excellent verse seems to result when requirements of the new form have been prepared for adequately in previous linguistic developments, inferior verse when prosodic requirements clash with linguistic possibilities. When Otfrid adopted rimed verse in the ninth century the rhythm of the language was still too irregular to yield alternating lines, nor had a stock of rimes been built up by predecessors. Three and one-half centuries later, after further linguistic changes leading to a regular alternating rhythm and a wide stock of rimes, and after the work of some capable predecessors, Gottfried von Strassburg, and on a somewhat lower level Wolfram von Eschenbach and Hartmann von der Ouwe, wrote excellent verse in essentially the same form as that Otfrid had imported. Far from ascribing this "efflorescence of verse" to the "invention or introduction of a new verse form" we must credit it rather to a combination of favorable linguistic and social conditions which were the culmination of years of development. When the Germanic languages had fully explored poetic components that did not clash with verse form but still permitted experimentation and enrichment by individual poets, when Germanic societies were deeply interested in verse and demanded of it the expression of their highest ideals, when foreign influences had been absorbed into native patterns, at such periods the Germanic peoples produced superior verse.

If we wish to learn the reasons for "efflorescence of verse," the history of verse form in more periods of flourishing poetry must be studied. "Academic critics" have unfortunately neglected in ever-greater measure linguistic study, leaving the study of verse form to "literary critics," such as Hulme and Edith Sitwell, whose conclusions are scarcely illuminating, as shown in the following comments from Miss Sitwell:[4]

The earliest English poetry of all, with its crude and unskilled thumping, or creaking, alliteration, echoes the sound of those earthy occupations which accompany the work of food-getting.

. . . the following magnificent line:
The mighty tresses in hir sonnish heres.

—I know, and have been reminded of the fact by correspondents, that the *o* in 'sonnish' was usually pronounced as the letter *u* is

[4] Edith Sitwell, *A Poet's Notebook* (London, 1944), 59, 61–62.

now pronounced in German. But variations were in use in the time of Chaucer, and I think that here is a case. If, then, 'sonnish' was pronounced as we now pronounce the word 'sun', each accented vowel-sound rises, sharply, after the other, springing upward.

Like every other human activity poetry must be studied in the context in which it is found. If one supposes that the ninth-century English spent all their waking hours hacking at underbrush or grinding corn, their poetry would also be beyond his comprehension. Nor is one who lacks an elementary understanding of linguistic activity qualified to contribute to the study of poetic form. If we are to understand the forces which produce excellent poetry, students with thorough linguistic and cultural backgrounds will have to investigate the external elements of great periods of poetry—the Elizabethan period and the periods of Goethe, Dante, Sophocles, Firdausi, and Li Po—and find the common external conditions. Poets themselves may then be able to suggest further special conditions which enable certain individuals to write superior verse. For one of the special conditions that does not yield to analysis is poetic genius, and this may enable its possessors to transcend conditions which seem generally valid.

Yet analytic work must be done by scholars, for poets seem unwilling or unable to detach themselves from poetry to analyze what are the exterior forces affecting their form. Eliot in his lecture *The Music of Poetry* leaves to historical scholars the problem of determining the influence of Latin poetry on Wyatt and Surrey, and is himself interested only in the results and their effects on subsequent verse, saying: "In the history of versification, the question whether poets have misunderstood the rhythms of the language in imitating foreign models does not arise: we must accept the practices of great poets of the past, because they are practices upon which our ear has been trained and must be trained." And Hopkins found evidence for sprung rhythm in Chaucer, but because he read him without pronouncing some final unaccented *e* vowels.[5] Since poets may accept uncritically the practices of their predecessors, it devolves on linguists to discover the forces which determine the poetic and linguistic rhythms of an author.

Linguists must undertake the study of poetry, for poetry is essentially a compact form of communication through language, and the techniques developed to study other forms of language can as readily be applied to poetry. Eliot's lines:

> The Chair she sat in, like a burnished throne,
> Glowed on the marble, where the glass
> Held up by standards wrought with fruited vines
> From which a golden Cupidon peeped out
> (Another hid his eyes behind his wing)
> Doubled the flames of sevenbranched candelabra
> Reflecting light upon the table as
> The glitter of her jewels rose to meet it,
> From satin cases poured in rich profusion; . . .

may be analyzed for play of sounds, rhythms, grammatical and stylistic form, imagery, and meaning. Such study has already been undertaken, notably by J. R. Firth.[6] But no less helpful to an understanding of verse will be the perspective given by comparative and historical study. After these lines are analyzed they may be compared with other lines of this passage, with other lines of this poem, with other lines of Eliot, and with other lines of English verse. Eliot's first line and next half-line are adapted from the *Antony and Cleopatra* passage cited above:

> The barge she sat in, like a burnish'd throne,
> Burn'd on the water: the poop was beaten gold;

[5] See W. H. Gardner, *Gerard Manley Hopkins* (2 vols., London, 1944–49), II, 166, fn. 1; but see also the reference there to a later letter.

[6] "Modes of Meaning," *Essays and Studies of the English Association* (1951), 118–49.

Purple the sails, and so perfumed that
The winds were love-sick with them; the oars were silver,
Which to the tune of flutes kept stroke and made
The water which they beat to follow faster,
As amorous of their strokes. For her own person,
It beggar'd all description : . . .

Rhythmical and grammatical comparison of the two passages shows that Shakespeare's rhythm is built up around short co-ordinate clauses, Eliot's on a long hypotactic construction. Both rhythm and grammatical construction underline the sense : the elation in *Antony and Cleopatra,* the boredom in *The Waste Land.* Possibly to the change in the English language between Shakespeare and Eliot as well as to the difference in mood we may attribute Eliot's substitution of *glowed* for *burned.* For Eliot's music is built on the vowels of *throne, glowed,* as much as on those of *burn-* and *burned,* while Shakespeare's music, as Stevenson pointed out, was constructed around the *ar, ur* sounds; *r* in these combinations had been lost before the time of Eliot's English in favor of long vowels. Yet only comprehensive study of Eliot could suggest what his rhythms are, and what are the causes of their difference from his predecessors'. For like all language, verse is a complex human activity and its changes are due to changes which may vary from poetry to poetry. If we wish to seek the causes for change in verse form in postmedieval poetry, we should have to take into account the influence of individual poets as well as those influences which we have found preeminent in the development of Germanic verse form : changes in language, in audience and presentation, and in direction of influence. Through investigation of these we have attempted to increase our understanding of Germanic poetry. Through investigation of the total number of forces at work at any time we should improve our understanding of a further poetic tradition, and of the linguistic achievement known as poetry.

INDEX

Note: Figures in italics refer to books, stanzas, and lines of poetry.